Go with

THE FLOW

LEARNING TO LIVE AND WORK OUT OF GOD'S ECONOMY

BY PETER J. BRISCOE

Published by: Compass - finances God's way
www.compass1.global

CONTENTS

THE AUTHOR

Peter Briscoe an Englishman, born in 1950, and studied Industrial Chemistry and Management at Loughborough University of Technology. He moved to The Netherlands in 1974 and was asked by his company to set up a subsidiary in Holland, selling chemical specialties to the aerospace and food processing industries. From 1986 to 2002, Peter was Executive Director of CBMC, Christian Businessmen's Committees, in Holland and Europe.

In 1990, Peter set up "Synthesys". a consulting company specialising in chemical product development. When the Berlin Wall collapsed in 1990, Peter developed Europartners, a movement dedicated to reaching European business and professional leaders for Christ.

From 2002, Peter took an assignment as Managing Director of HE Space Operations, serving the European Space institutions, specialising in providing professional services for spaceflight activities. In that time, he co-founded the International Association for the Advancement of Space Safety.

From 2008, Peter retired from business to develop a movement of Biblical stewardship in Europe, first of all as International VP of Crown Financial Ministries and then as European director of Compass - finances God's way. Peter was a co-founder of the European Economic Summit.

At home, Peter is Chair of the Church board of the Baptist Church of Leiden. He is married to his Dutch wife, Didie since 1972. They are blessed with three daughters and six grandchildren.

INTRODUCTION

This book is called, "The Flow," because learning to live and work in God's economy is like allowing yourself to be carried along by the flow of the Spirit, leading and guiding you through the economy of the world in which we live. The economy of the kingdom of God is not a structure to be built, but a stream of God's activity to be experienced. It is my prayer that you experience being carried along on streams of Living Water, which bring life into the world in which God has placed us.

A practical example is the longest river in the world, the Nile. It was so important for the Egyptians that they dubbed the river 'River God' and the area where the Nile floods to fertilize the crops their land they called the 'Black Land' and the rest was the 'Red Land' – the desert. The rich, Black Land represented life. The arid Red Land meant danger. For Egyptians, the Nile literally meant the difference between life and death. When the river overflows, the land can bring forth fruit! It is the same for us; when the life of Christ in a person or group overflows, fruit will grow.

There is a subtle temptation that encourages Christians to try to do God's work in man's way. 'Getting results' becomes the primary focus. It almost seems that we believe that the end justifies the means. An examination of God's Word shows that the means are sometimes even more important than the results. The world tries to convince you that as long as you can accomplish something for the kingdom of God, that's all that matters. For example, Ananias and Sapphira gave an offering to their church, which was a good thing, but they did it deceitfully. God judged them immediately, not for what they did, but for how they did it[1].

Satan tried to trap Jesus with this same temptation. Satan did not question the worthiness of Jesus' task, but simply offered 'practical' solutions to accomplish Jesus' goal more quickly and at lesser cost. He was offered security, provision and power if only He would accept Satan's authority. God's ways are not like man's ways. 'Efficiency' from man's perspective is not prized by God. It did not seem efficient to have the children of Israel march around Jericho thirteen times and then blow their trumpets, but it brought the walls down[2]. It did not appear wise to select the youngest of Jesse's sons to become the next king, but God saw a man after His own heart[3]. At first glance, it does not seem logical for Jesus to have picked that strange collection of men as His disciples, yet through them God dramatically affected their world.

It is never wise to attempt to do God's work in man's way. It is an age-old temptation that seems to make sense on the surface but often is at variance with the purposes of God.

Solutions to working and living in Gods economy can only be found in the context of a living, daily relationship with the Lord and allowing the Holy Spirit to take us along on the flow of the Kingdom. Living and working in God/s economy is a journey, not a destination.

I would like to get us going on a journey to understand the way God is thinking about economics ... and new challenges require a new way of thinking. This book is designed, not to give ideas for a new economic system, because the economy of the Kingdom of God can never be captured by a system; it is more like a dynamic river, carrying us along on our journey; and God's Word is a compass

---

1. Acts 5:1-11
2. Joshua 6
3. 1 Samuel 16:11

helping us to navigate the waters.

In this book, we will discuss ways in which the flow of the economy of the Kingdom of God can influence our worldly economy; how can we ensure the gospel of the Kingdom can permeate our earthly systems in order that we can fulfil the great commandments as Jesus taught - to love God above all, and our neighbours as ourselves. The economy of the Kingdom of God has to be applicable in order to fulfil the great commission which Jesus gave us to "Go and make disciples of all nations ... teaching them to obey all I have commanded you[4]."

Let's go with the flow of the economy of the Kingdom of God!

---

4. Matthew 28:18-20

YOUR KINGDOM COME

Writing on the Economy of the Kingdom is a daunting task! That the Kingdom of God has its own economy with its own characteristics is not evident to many.

The very different economics of the Kingdom are illustrated by some Bible verses such as the words spoken to Joshua on entering the promised land, "So I gave you a land on which you did not toil and cities you did not build; and you live in them and eat from vineyards and olive groves that you did not plant[1]." The invitation given by God Himself seems not to make sense in today's economy; "Come, all you who are thirsty, come to the waters; and you who have no money, come, buy and eat! Come, buy wine and milk without money and without cost. Why spend money on what is not bread, and your labour on what does not satisfy[2]?" This only happens when the flow of God's economy permeates the world's economy.

The early church illustrated the coming of the economics of the Kingdom. "Now the full number of those who believed were of one heart and soul, and no one said that any of the things that belonged to him was his own, but they had everything in common. And with great power the apostles were giving their testimony to the resurrection of the Lord Jesus, and great grace was upon them all. There was not a needy person among them, for as many as were

---

1. Joshua24:13
2. Isaiah 53:1,2

owners of lands or houses sold them and brought the proceeds of what was sold and laid it at the apostles' feet, and it was distributed to each as any had need. Thus Joseph, who was also called by the apostles Barnabas (which means son of encouragement), a Levite, a native of Cyprus, sold a field that belonged to him and brought the money and laid it at the apostles' feet."[3]

Acquisition without paying, buying with no money, provision of needs, elimination of poverty, liberal sharing, asset distribution … does this sound good?

Your will be done on Earth

"Your Kingdom come—Your will be done on earth as it is in heaven."

The Kingdom of God is a society upon earth where Gods will is perfectly done as it is in heaven and which exists in the past, present and future all at the one time.

To be in the Kingdom is to obey the will of God. The Kingdom is not something which primarily has to do with nations and peoples and countries. It is something which has to do with each one of us. The Kingdom is in fact the most personal thing in the world. The Kingdom demands the submission of my will, my heart, my life. It is only when each one of us makes this personal decision and submission that the Kingdom comes.

The Chinese Christian prayed the well-known prayer, "Lord, revive thy Church, beginning with me," and we might well paraphrase that and say, "Lord, bring in thy Kingdom, beginning with me." To pray for the Kingdom of Heaven is to pray that we may submit our wills entirely to the will of God.

The starting point for living and working in Gods economy is submission. Like baptism, it is to be immersed in the dynamic flow of the Trinity, to submit my will to His will and allow myself to be

---

3. 7. Acts 4:32-37

carried along by the Spirit.

Well, we pray every day to God that; "Your will be done on earth … as it is in heaven." Therefore, the ways and means of heaven should also become applicable to our earthly economy! Gods economy is an 'inside-out' economy,' whereby God is influencing the earthly economy through his children.

As it is in Heaven?

Jesus shows us what God is doing, is moving us steadily toward His ultimate goal, which is described in the last book of the Bible, Revelation: "Look! God's dwelling place is now among the people, and He will dwell with them. They will be His people, and God Himself will be with them and be their God. He will wipe every tear from their eyes. There will be no more death or mourning or crying or pain, for the old order of things has passed away."

God's dwelling place right now is in you and me. We are moving with the flow towards the perfect state of the economy of the Kingdom which will only become reality in the new order.

There will be a maximum abundance of every capital, of which I believe there are five major types.

Spiritual — God dwelling among His people, and His people knowing Him completely and cooperating with Him fully.

Relational — No more war or conflict between people; instead, perfect relational harmony and peace.

Physical — No more death or sickness; instead, perfect health for our bodies and environment.

Productive — Creativity and ideas abound. (You didn't think heaven would be boring, did you?)

Financial — No more poverty or lack of any kind, indeed no money, but sharing an abundance of everything needed for a full life.

This isn't some kind of private enrichment programme—it's how we participate with God in what he's doing in the world. God's purpose is for everyone to share in an abundance of spiritual capital, which causes flourishing in all the other areas of capital. God's heart is for the holistic flourishing of his people right now - today - in all these five areas of capital.

Jesus taught us to pray for God's kingdom to come (here), for His will to be done on earth as it is in heaven (now). The flourishing of heaven is meant to touch our lives, working places and our neighbourhoods today!

The way that God achieves this goal is, remarkably, through his people. God has invested in us, and like the master in the parable of the talents, He is looking for a return on that investment, desiring that it will bear fruit and grow and be invested in others for the flourishing of all humanity. The return God gets on His investment is that more and more people come to know Him and begin to function as humans were meant to function, prospering in all of the five capitals and investing in others so they too can prosper. God's heart from the very beginning has been the blessing of all people, the flourishing of humanity.

Influencing

Israel's Jordan River is a 156-mile-long river that flows north to south from the Sea of Galilee to the Dead Sea. It remains a source of life as it flows into the Sea of Galilee and then travels to the Dead Sea. Throughout history, towns and cities have been situated on the sea, and it has served as a centre of trade. Fish and plant life are abundant in the area. In all likelihood, Paul witnessed first-hand the Sea of Galilee's generous irrigation as well as abundant fishing resources. In the Gospels, Jesus and the disciples travel by boat all around the Sea of Galilee, meeting people, fishing its waters and participating in the local culture.

Today, the Sea of Galilee is just as active and populated as a regional centre of commerce and tourism and is surrounded by farms, resorts and bustling communities.

In contrast, the Dead Sea has no outlet, greedily robbing the arid region of moisture. It's a lake in which nothing swims or grows. It is extremely salty and is a harsh environment in which animals, plants and other aquatic organisms cannot flourish. In Hebrew prose, it is simply called the 'Sea of Death' due to its scarcity of life. While there are small settlements near the Dead Sea and its extreme mineral traits have been found to have therapeutic qualities that draw a niche crowd, overall it is no hub like the Sea of Galilee.

So, what's the difference? Both seas are fed by the same river. It is only when the waters are active and moving that they retain their productive, community-building value. The Sea of Galilee gives back out what it is receiving from the Jordan River, while the Dead Sea is just a dead end, and every drop it gets, it keeps. Once the Jordan River's fresh waters stop flowing and come to a halt, they become stale and salty and lose their abilities to sustain life.

Many aspects of our economy are like the Dead Sea. It takes the plentiful resources and hoards them, stores them and benefits only the few. Greed has become the norm in our capitalist economy. Someone said it is like a canning factory. 'Get all you can, can what you get and then sit on the can.' Accumulation leads to stagnation. Greed causes the flow to stop and the economy becomes dead. Sharing causes the flow to bring life. Greed causes our lives to also become foul before God. But a life that flows abundantly shares all that God has given us. When we give, we truly prosper and are refreshed.[4]

If we act out of our abundance and keep resources moving for the enrichment of all around us, the value to us and to others can multiply beyond what we could ever imagine and supply life and joy to those with whom we come into contact.

---

4. 8. Proverbs 11:24,25

The Okavango River

One of my most endearing memories of my visits to Africa, was some days spent in Botswana in the Okavango Delta. Meandering from the Angolan highlands, through Namibia, all the way to Botswana, is the Okavango River.

Looking at a satellite image you can easily see snaking blue lines as this magnificent river spreads into an alluvial basin in the middle of one of the world's biggest stretches of sand. It is a truly magical experience visiting this oasis in a desert, but the true magic lies in timing a visit to coincide with the coming of the winter floods.

These floods allow a vibrant ecosystem to thrive. The process begins when the summer rainfalls from the Angola highlands (January–February) drain into the Okavango River and is then spread over the delta over the next four months (March–June). This flooding is known to attract the greatest concentrations of wildlife in Africa, which is most evident during the flood peaks between June and August, during Botswana's dry winter months.

During this time of much anticipated relief, the delta comes to life as the delta swells to three times its permanent size. As the floodplains spread, the results are almost immediately evident – green plants begin to shoot, antelope give birth and the once dull, brown landscape turns to an unimaginable palette of green colours.

The traditional greeting of Botswana is "GOROGA ka pula" —"Welcome with the rain." This fits so well, because this is a hot, dusty, semiarid country where rain means so much to life. After the flooding season, the waters in the lower parts of the delta recede, leaving moisture behind in the soil.

This residual moisture is used for planting fodder and other crops that can thrive on it.

The economy of the Kingdom can bring life to a sometimes dry and barren economy and promote life as God intended.

The Gulf Stream

The Gulf Stream is one of the most closely studied ocean currents in the world, because scientists consider it so important to the transport of heat around the world. Sometimes the Gulf Stream is so strong that it is possible to see it from space.

The Gulf Stream is the reason why Norway and Northern Europe have a relatively mild climate. It brings water that has been heated up by the powerful sun in the Gulf of Mexico, and splits into several branches that distribute the Caribbean warmth throughout Northern Europe. The Gulf Stream transports 50 million cubic meters of water per second, which is more than all of the world's rivers put together.

Though Scotland is on the same latitude as Siberia, palm trees grow on some Scottish islands. Northern parts of Norway lie close to the Arctic zone, most of which is covered with ice and snow in winter. However, almost all of Norway's coast remains free of ice and snow throughout the year. Though it makes a journey of thousands of miles from the Gulf, the Gulf Stream continues to bring warmth and life!

Billy Graham likened the effect of the Kingdom to the Gulf Stream. In a 1968 rally he said, 'Christians are like the gulf stream, which is in the ocean and yet not part of it. This mysterious current defies the mighty Atlantic, ignores its tides, and flows steadily upon its course. Its colour is different, being a deeper blue. Its temperature is different, being warmer. Its direction is different, being from south to north. It is in the ocean, and yet it is not part of it.

So we as Christians are in the world. We come in contact with the world, and yet we retain our distinctive kingdom character and refuse to let the world press us into its mould.

The world is keenly aware of its emptiness, of its unfulfilled dreams, of its failure to cope with life. The world system is inadequate to meet the deeper needs of the human heart. These are ideal waters in which to inject the Gospel. God has seen fit to entrust the work of

His kingdom to us. If the world system is changed, it will be through the life-giving stream of the Kingdom of God.

We are clearly to be in the world, but not a part of it. The influence of Christians, led by the Holy Spirit, is to be a stream of 'living water,' permeating the economy with the economy of the Kingdom.

THE PROBLEMS

When writing this, the experiences of the global economic crisis of 2007-2015 are still very fresh in my mind. Charles Kindleberger, a financial historian, studied four centuries of banking events and concluded that financial crises occur on average about every 10 years. In relatively recent times, the 1970s featured real estate credit crises in both Britain and the US and what was then called 'The Great Recession.'

The 1980s brought the global crisis of imploding loans to the governments of less-developed countries, as well as the failure of the remarkable total of more than 2.500 US financial institutions between 1982 and 1992. In the 1990s, there were a series of international financial crises: Mexico, Russia and in Asia, as well as the creation of the US tech stock bubble, which shrivelled early in 2000. The 2000s of course brought the collapse of multiple national housing bubbles, a European sovereign debt crisis and another 'Great Recession,' from 2008 to 2015. Paul Volcker, chairman of the American FED, wittily remarked that 'about every 10 years, we have the greatest crisis in 50 years.'

Lessons from the crisis

What lessons can we learn from these crises? We have learnt some important lessons. Together, these are a profound shock to the philosophical and economic assumptions that have underpinned the West for the last 25 years.

Here is a list of seven lessons, given by a well-known banker in the City of London.

1. We are more prone to temptation than we thought. If left to our own devices, we often do not behave either rationally or well. Deregulation has proven to be unwise. The 'invisible hand' of the market has not guided us so well! However, we have learned that regulation alone is not enough. Passing more laws does not deliver responsible behaviour any more than it delivers profitable business.

2. We have learned that people who are solely focussed on money become greedy, narcissistic, and individualistic.

A businessman came to a rabbi asking for advice. The rabbi asked, "Look through the window, tell me, what do you see?"

"Well. I see the world... trees, grass, flowers... a beautiful view," replied the businessman.

"Now look at this mirror... what do you see now?"

"I see only myself."

"That's what happens when your world view is coated with silver... you see only yourself.

3. We have been unable to deal with greed! This greed has alienated us from business leaders who line their own pockets while laying off hundreds of their employees; leaders who receive salaries hundreds of times greater than their employees. From bankers who leave unsuccessful banks with large bonuses to politicians who choose corruption rather than honesty.

4. We are not as clever as we thought. We have created 'expert' structures we do not understand and cannot control, and we have realised that the future is more uncertain than we

imagined. We have seen the death of the Expert! When hauled up before a Congressional committee to explain the payment of huge wages and bonuses to top executives, the CEO of a large car manufacturer gave as a reason, "We need to pay such packages in order to attract the best industry experts." A congressman quipped, "Look at the crisis you are in. You have no experts." The financial world has devised such complicated derivatives that no-one understands what's going on. Someone said there are only 75 people in the world who know what all these exotic financial derivatives are!

5.   The prosperity of each of us is more connected to the well-being of others than we thought, rather than money or possessions... 'the pursuit of profit as an end in itself has led to individualism and this by definition destroys relationships.'

6.   Maximisation of shareholder value as a strategy for business has contributed to the problem, not solved it... when focused only on money, people are relegated to the second place, and become eventually means to an end - not the end themselves! Pope Francis said on the Davos web site, "Humanity must be served by wealth, not ruled by it."

7.   The market does not protect us from disaster and, when economic shocks do occur, the market will not save us.

These lessons have left us in uncharted waters with no reliable means of navigation. They have ignited, for the first time in a generation, real interest in discussing the best principles upon which to base national and international business and finance.

How can we avoid making the same mistakes in the future? Einstein famously quoted, "We cannot solve problems using the same thinking that originally caused the problems in the first place." How can we think differently about personal and corporate finance in a vulnerable economy? It has been said that money will not solve financial problems - it will only alleviate the symptoms for a short time - and that the financial crises we experience, are at the core, a problem of the human heart, not a technical problem. We need a new way of thinking, both collectively and individually, which changes our behaviour.

We know we should not go back to how things were before, although the danger remains that we will. Let us be honest enough to examine the personal shortcomings and structural difficulties that had locked us into a system that doesn't deliver. We can no longer allow the system to drive our values. Our values must now drive the system.

It is not often that quite so many of us have failed to make the right choices, and seldom have so many failed – quite comprehensively – the test of both character and competence.

We need to look ahead and consider the lessons arising from crises and we need to decide how to build a prosperous and sustainable future for all of us.

No lessons learned.

I read an interesting book recently by Joris Luyendijk, a Dutch journalist working for the Guardian newspaper in London. He interviewed many top- and middle level executives in the City of London, trying to understand how the financial system works, and if there have been any lessons learned from the past 7 years of crisis. The bottom-line? He maintains that no lessons were learned at all! It is business as usual. He wrote, "If you had described the effects of the crisis to anyone in 2008 and said that 7 years later nothing had changed, no-one would believe you."

The only thing the bankers have learned is that they can get away with anything!

A banker's oath was introduced. Luyendijk was very sceptical about this. "What you are doing is maintaining the temptations for them. You are saying, 'Children, here is a box of sweets and I am leaving the room. I want you to promise not to touch them.' We have learned from 2008 on that bankers cannot control themselves."

I found some of his comments about Christians in the banking world disturbing. Luyendijk said in an interview with a major Dutch daily, "Bankers have delegated their conscience to the law-giver. If it is permissible it's ok. Good and evil do not play any part on the banking floor. Developing a new, risky financial product is possible so long as the law allows it. We would never introduce a medicine in that way!"

The financial world uses us as 'Guinee pigs' to try out new instruments. Luyendijk went on to say, "The Christians, Jews and Muslims I spoke to are very good in compartmentalising. They are people with a highly developed ethical awareness, but when they enter the bank, it is like they enter a spaceship where other norms apply."

Compartmentalisation is a danger to all Christians and a common problem. When the Titanic was built, they thought that it's 6 compartments would hold any water which may get into one or more of them. It didn't work. The water flowed from one to another and the ship sank. Ethical behaviour cannot be compartmentalised - it will flow from one part of my life to the next. That is integrity - that all parts behave in the same way.

I saw an intriguing title of a book about the financial crisis, written by two members of the House of Commons in the UK parliament. "Masters of Nothing: How The Crash Will Happen Again Unless We Understand Human Nature." There is no better source to understand human nature than the Bible. Paul wrote to his disciple Timothy, "For the time is coming when people will not endure sound teaching, but having itching ears they will accumulate for themselves teachers to suit their own passions, and will turn away from listening to the truth and wander off into myths.[1]"

Albert Einstein was heard to say, "Only two things are infinite, the universe and human stupidity, and I'm not sure about the former."

---

1. 2 Timothy 4:3

Sadly, it does seem that far too often there is no limit to the foolishness we get ourselves into—or the damage we create by our foolishness and the choices it fosters.

The answer to such destructive foolishness is to embrace the wisdom of God. Only by allowing God to transform us can we overcome the foolish decisions that cause so much trouble. With His loving guidance, we can follow the pathway of godly wisdom.

Apocalypse now!

So, after the last crisis, no lessons have really been learned! It is business as usual again!" A leading figure in our economy echoed what I have heard from several commentators about lessons learned from the last crisis period.

The former Chief Economist of the World Bank, Joseph Stieglitz, wrote an article for Vanity Fair magazine in which he used a cartoon by Edward Sorel, depicting four horsemen responsible for bringing chaos and crisis to our economy, inspired by the apocalyptic horsemen from the Bible book of Revelation.

The real forces behind global economic trends are essentially spiritual, matters affecting the human heart - and this was certainly so for the last crisis period. The four heart issues which Sorel depicted are: Deception, Stupidity, Arrogance and Greed; issues which are still affecting our economy today!

1. Deception, is rife. Just think of identity theft, mail fraud, and business deceit such as falsifying software to achieve certain desired results (VW Diesel-gate). Deception is rife in government, when our leaders break promises, hide costs and spin arguments ... Jeremiah tells us, "The heart is deceitful above all things, and desperately sick; who can understand it?[2]" Solomon gives us the antidote; "The integrity of the

---

2. Jeramiah 17:9

upright guides them, but the crookedness of the treacherous destroys them.[3]"

2. Stupidity. We seem to fall so easily for all kind of attractive schemes - 'get-rich-quick,' pyramid schemes always find plenty of investors. Our economic schemes are so complex that even those who devised them in the first place lose their understanding of what is going on!

3. One of the most influential economists, Friedrich Hayek, gave us a reality check on our abilities … with this challenge! "The curious task or economics is to demonstrate to men how little they really know about what they imagine they can design." In 1968 he wrote, 'Modern civilisation has given man undreamt of powers largely because, without understanding it, he has developed methods of utilising more knowledge and resources than any one mind is aware of.' On the title page of his book, he states; "man has become all he is without understanding what happened." Pursuing profit maximisation leads ultimately to chaos and crisis!

4. Paul warned Timothy, "But those who desire to be rich fall into temptation, into a snare, into many senseless and harmful desires that plunge people into ruin and destruction. For the love of money is a root of all kinds of evils. It is through this craving that some have wandered away from the faith and pierced themselves with many pangs.[4]"

5. Arrogance. Money gives people power and controls others; suppliers, employees, debtors and others around you. Power corrupts and wielding the power of money can lead to arrogance, a feeling of superiority and a detachment from reality. Paul again, "As for the rich in this present age, charge them not to be haughty, nor to set their hopes on the uncertainty of riches, but on God, who richly provides us

---

3. Proverbs 11:3
4. 1 Timothy 6:10

with everything to enjoy."

6. Greed. This is the most quoted of the root causes of the last crisis. Prof. Tomas Sedlacek, Czech economist, says, "The more we have, the more we want. Why? Perhaps we thought (and this sounds truly intuitive) that the more we have, the less we will need. We thought that consumption would lead to saturation of our needs. But the opposite has proven to be true. The more we have, the more additional things we need. Every new satisfied want will beget a new one and will leave us wanting. For consumption is like a drug."

7. Paul gave Timothy the antidote to greed ..."They are to do good, to be rich in good works, to be generous and ready to share, thus storing up treasure for themselves as a good foundation for the future, so that they may take hold of that which is truly life."

We can defeat the four horsemen of the Apocalypse! Following Jesus and obeying His words will enable us to turn things around. Instead of deception - integrity; instead of stupidity - wisdom; instead of arrogance - humility; instead of greed - generosity.

Something is broken

I saw the movie, Wall Street 2 with increasing recognition that this represented what has been going on since Wall Street 1 was made in the late eighties. One of the best scenes was when Gordon Gecko was giving a lecture to some students about greed. What this ex Wall Street insider did in about three minutes, was to describe the cause of the 2007 - 2015 financial crisis almost poetically. It was a bit dramatic, but it was one of the best explanations for the financial crisis in summary form. I have tried to relay here what he said in the film.

Gordon Gecko shakes his head and says:

"You are all pretty much screwed. You do not know it yet, but you are the NINJA generation; No income, no job, no assets. You've got a lot to look forward to!

Someone reminded me the other day that I once said, greed is good. Well it appears greed is not only good, it is legal. We are all drinking the same cool-aid.

But it is greed that makes my bartender buy three houses he cannot afford, with no money down. And it is greed that makes your parents refinance their 200,000 dollar mortgage for 250,000 dollars. Now they take that extra 50,000 dollars and go to the shopping mall so they can buy a new plasma TV, cell phones, computers and an SUV. And hey, why not a second home while we are at it.

> Gee Wiz, we all know the prices of houses in America always go up. Right?

> It is greed that makes the government of this country cut the interest rates to 1% after 9/11 so we can all go shopping again.

> They got all these fancy names for trillions of dollars for credit, CMO, CDO, SIV, ABS. You know I honestly think there are only 75 people in the world that know what they are.

> But I will tell you what they are, they are WMDs. Weapons of mass destruction.

> When I was away, it seemed that greed, got greedier. With a little bit of envy mixed in.

> Hedge fund managers came home with 50 to 100 million bucks a year.

> So Mr. Banker, he looks around and says.

My life looks pretty boring.

So he starts leveraging his interest up to 40%, 50% to 100%. With your money, not his. Yours! Because he could.

You are supposed to be borrowing, not them.

And the beauty of the deal is no one is responsible.

Because everyone is drinking the same cool-aid.

Last year ladies and gentlemen, 40% of all corporate profits came from the financial services industry.

Not production, not anything remotely to do with the needs of the American public.

The truth is we are all part of it now.

Banks, consumers they are moving the money around in circles.

We take a buck; we shoot it full of steroids and we call it leverage. I call it steroid banking.

Now I have been considered a pretty smart guy when it comes to finance.

Maybe I was in prison too long, but sometimes it is the only place to stay sane, looking out from the bars and say, hey is everyone out there nuts?

It is clear as a bell to those who pay attention. The mother of all evil is speculation. Leverage debt. The bottom line is, it is borrowing to the hilt.

And I hate to tell you this, but it is a bankrupt business model.

It will not work. It is septicemic, malignant and its global. Like cancer, it is a disease. And we got to fight back. How we going to do that?

How we are going to leverage that disease, back in our favour?"

Greed is never good, nor does it serve to work any good purpose. Since we will never be able to attain everything we desire, greed offers us dissatisfaction. Our greediness ultimately destroys us as we harden our hearts, ignoring the needs of others. Ultimately, greed motivates us to pursue poor choices that plunge us into destruction

While few of us are millionaires, it is easy to fall victim to greed. When our yearning for another's possessions takes seed, we produce covetousness. Our materialism becomes insatiable as we attempt to acquire objects that are upgraded or more impressive than our neighbour's.

Greed is like producing a Dead Sea. Generosity and sharing brings life.

The Philosopher's stone

From the Middle Ages to the late 17th-century, the so-called 'philosopher's stone' was the most sought-after goal in the world of alchemy, the medieval ancestor of chemistry. According to legend, the philosopher's stone was a substance that could turn ordinary metals such as iron, tin, lead, zinc, nickel or copper into precious metals like gold and silver. It also acted as an elixir of life, with the power to cure illness, renew the properties of youth and even grant immortality to those who possessed it.

The Bank of England was created in 1694 by a Scotsman, William Paterson, who famously said: "The bank has benefit of interest on all moneys which it creates out of nothing." Today, our banks are enjoying the philosopher's stone which they have created. Megabucks out of nothing but megabytes!

It is said that at the incorporation of the Bank of England, it was promised, "We will provide unlimited financial means - in return, we will keep the absolute privilege to create money." (To be precise:

false money - or what the banks call fiat money!) Fiat money is money that has value only because of government regulation or law. The term derives from the Latin 'fiat', meaning 'let it be done.' Fiat money is the opposite of honest money. Fiat money is money that is declared to have value even if it does not. There begins the deception!

About a hundred years later, the influential German author Goethe, tells the story of a young scholar, Faust, who enters into a pact with the devil in the form of his ally Mephistopheles. In return for Mephistopheles' services to help him realise his ambitions, Faust makes a pact with the devil and pledges his soul.

In the Second Part of Faust, Faust attends the court of a ruler whose empire is facing financial ruin because of government overspending. (Sound familiar?) Rather than urging the emperor to be more financially responsible, Mephistopheles—disguised as a court jester—suggests a different approach, one with disturbing parallels to our own age.

Noting that the empire's currency is gold, Mephistopheles maintains there is surely plenty of undiscovered gold underneath the earth belonging to the emperor. Thus, he argues, the emperor can issue promissory notes for the value of this yet-to-be-found gold, thereby generating fresh monetary resources for the government and solving its debt problems.

The emperor and his treasurer are delighted with this idea. It means the monarch can avoid making hard economic choices while simultaneously providing the empire with desperately needed currency. Mephistopheles subsequently deluges the court with paper money, and Faust is praised by emperor and commoner alike.

The results, however, are not what are expected. First, the issuance of paper money does not solve the emperor's spending problems. Instead the ruler and his court become even more extravagant, knowing they can always print more paper money to cover their ever-growing expenses. Second, the devil through his ally Mephistopheles, has subtly but fundamentally changed the basis of the empire's currency.

Instead of being rooted in the solidity offered by a tangible and valued asset, the currency is now based on flimsy paper promises. Thus, long-term monetary stability and powerful restraints on extravagant government spending are sacrificed for short-term gain.

Goethe finished writing the second part of Faust in 1832, yet Goethe's insights go to the heart of some of our most intractable long-term economic problems.

Jesus unmasked the real power behind money when He said, "You cannot serve both God and mammon." Goethe adequately described the work of mammon in our economy through his character Mephistopheles. This caused over-indulgence, overspending, loss of trust and financial chaos.

Today we have the creation of free money - money has never been so cheap. From an economic perspective, the printing press is not necessary, as the creation of money primarily shows up electronically on the central bank's balance sheet, on its accounts.

If central banks can potentially create an unlimited amount of money out of thin air, how can we ensure that money remains sufficiently scarce to preserve its value? Does this ability to create money more or less at will not create the temptation to take advantage of this instrument to create additional leeway short term, even at the risk of highly probable long-term damage?

Yes, this temptation certainly does exist, and many in monetary history have succumbed to it. Taking a look back in time, this was often the reason for establishing a central bank: to provide those in power with free access to seemingly unlimited financial resources.

So, what is the solution? A strong economy in which money plays its part as a medium of exchange, can only be built on what God has created - human, natural and relational capital. That is, land, agriculture, real resources such as precious metals and the honest, industrial application of human talent and ingenuity to create value.

The problem with GDP

It is vital to understand that the world's economic situation is made up by Real Economy and Financial Economy. The Real Economy is the world's combined GDP, the value of all private and public production and services. Globally, this represents a meagre 7 % of the total, while the Financial Economy represents 93 % of the total. (Currency exchange not included.)

Our economic system is a house of cards. Debt, both household and national is still increasing rapidly. A house built on a foundation of paper is a crisis waiting to happen.

Measuring our economies' value by gross domestic product falls short. According to Robert Kennedy, "GDP measures neither the health of our children, or quality of our education, nor the joy of their play. It measures neither the beauty of our poetry, nor the strength of our marriages. It pays no heed to the intelligence of our public debate, or the integrity of our public officials. It measures neither our wisdom nor our learning, neither our wit nor our courage, neither our compassion nor our devotion to country. It measures everything, in short, except that which makes life worth living, and it can tell us everything about our country except those things that make me proud to be a part of it".

We need a new way of evaluating our economy - God's way.

Complexity

This recession, from 2008 on, announced the death of the expert! Things have got so complex that we are no longer able to control them. I heard this comment from a respected German professor in economics. "Our autonomous intelligence is permanently creating systems of such a high degree of complexity, that our learning and controlling capabilities are getting increasingly overstretched." He then went on to quote from Romans. "Because men refused to recognise God and take Him seriously, God gave them over to their corrupt and disqualified minds." He summarised this as, "Man is too stupid for his own intelligence!"

The more power economists and politicians have, the more decisions are made, the more meetings they have in Jackson Hole, and Davos, Switzerland, the more meetings they have of G-20s and G-10s, the more rules they impose, the more chaotic financial markets become. If somebody tries to rule the world in place of God in the name of stability, they do not produce stability. They produce chaos. We are living in the age of financial chaos because we gave in to the men who said, "Treat me like a god and I will give you stability."

At this moment in history, when 'Davos Man' is failing so miserably that now it's almost impossible for even their most ardent cult-members to say, "Davos will save us! The planners will save us! The Keynesian elites will save us!" How devout can you be before eventually you say, 'Okay, that's not going to work?'

The answer to such destructive foolishness is to embrace the wisdom of God. Solomon reminds us, "The fear of the Lord is the beginning of wisdom, and the knowledge of the Holy One is understanding.[5]" Only by allowing God to transform us can we overcome the foolish decisions that cause so much trouble. With His loving guidance, we can follow the flowing river of godly wisdom.

---

5. Proverbs 9:10

NEW THINKING NEEDED

Our world view determines the nature of our economy. As we approach economics, as any area of life, we all start with presuppositions. Our presuppositions or set of ideas and beliefs that we hold about the world, will determine how we view economics, and hence, how we as a people organise our economic systems and policies (as well as our governmental systems, which have a great impact upon our economic systems).

Christians start with the idea that GOD IS. Non-believers should also, since this forms the foundation for prosperity and liberty. C.H. MacIntosh wonderfully compared non-believers' and believers' approach to knowledge, writing in 1882. "He [the non-believer] measures everything by his own standard and rejects whatever he cannot reconcile with his own notions. He lays down, with marvellous coolness, his own premises, and then proceeds to draw his own conclusions; but if the premises are false, the conclusions must be false likewise. And there is this invariable feature attaching to the premises of all sceptics, rationalists, and infidels—they always leave out God; and hence all their conclusions must be fatally false. On the other hand, the humble believer starts with this great first principle, that God is; and not only that He is, but that He has to do with His creatures; that He interests Himself in, and occupies Himself about, the affairs of men."

We start with the premise that there is a God Who created all things, including man—and God is concerned about the economy, about how we manage our household and our nation. Viewing man from God's perspective has great implications for economics. The Christian view of man includes:

- Man is created in the image of God, and hence has great value.

- Man has many characteristics of his Creator, including the ability to choose.

GOD IS and He has revealed Himself in His Word. He has also revealed principles for all of life (including economy). Christians must reason from those principles to obtain the fruit of obedience and influence the world's economy.

Thinking differently

We need to develop a Biblical way of thinking about our economy because times change. The message of the Bible is unchanging and remains steady as a rock in stormy seas. Times change, and we go from boom to bust so very quickly. We are faced with new problems on a daily basis.

Biblical thinking was demonstrated by the two spies, Joshua and Caleb, who in a team of twelve went into the new land to determine Israel's chances of entering. Ten came back with the report that the cities were impregnable, and that the inhabitants looked like giants. "In our eyes we look like grasshoppers[1]." Their way of thinking was fatalistic and not in faith. Joshua and Caleb gave their report. "If the Lord delights in us, he will bring us into this land and give it to us, a land that flows with milk and honey. Only do not rebel against the Lord. And do not fear the people of the land, for they are bread for us. Their protection is removed from them, and the Lord is with us; do not fear them[2]." Their worldview was one of faith in a God for whom nothing is impossible. Their attitude was that the perceived

---

1. Joshua 13:33
2. Joshua 14:8,9

problems were there for eating, like their daily bread on which they live! Their way of thinking was 'opportunities are wrapped-up in problems' and it's up to us to unwrap the tough circumstances which envelope us and use the opportunities inside.

J.F. Kennedy is quoted as saying, "When written in Chinese, the word 'crisis' is composed of two characters —one represents danger, and the other represents opportunity."

World principles

When thinking about how to influence the world economy with the principles of the Kingdom, we need to realise that there are spiritual forces at work which influence our thinking.

Paul wrote, "Beware lest anyone cheat you through philosophy and empty deceit, according to the tradition of men, according to the basic principles of the world, and not according to Christ[3]."

Elsewhere, Paul writes that our battle is "not against flesh and blood[4]," but against the 'arguments' that are arrogant and contrary to the knowledge of God[5]. The Greek word Paul uses here is '*logismoi*', which are sinful systems of thought, evil ways of life, and religious but anti-Christian principles which promise meaning, hope, and protection. '*Logismoi* 'are worldviews that shape the economy. They are social idols that capture the economy and form overarching sinful narratives on which people rely.

Paul in writing to his friends in Corinth, which was a large, economically very successful city, gave the answer to dealing with this way of thinking. "For though we live in the world, we do not wage war as the world does. The weapons we fight with are not the weapons of the world. On the contrary, they have divine power to demolish strongholds. We demolish arguments and every pretension

3. Colossians 2:8
4. Ephesians 6:12
5. 2 Corinthians 10:5

that sets itself up against the knowledge of God, and we take captive every thought to make it obedient to Christ[6]."

The weapons which Paul is talking about are the elements of the spiritual armour of God, described in Ephesians 5. The belt of truth will counter lies and false notions. The breastplate of righteousness protects against the counter-current of subtle temptations. The gospel of peace brings shalom, healing and wholeness to people and their relationships. The shield of faith helps us overcome spiritual attacks, so we can follow Gods will. The helmet of salvation will protect our reasoning and godly thinking. The sword of the Spirit is God's Word and we can use this to attack false doctrines and equip ourselves to do good work. Interestingly, there is no armour mentioned for our back … and we need each other to cover us!

A new paradigm

My goal is to help you on a journey to understand the way God is thinking about economics … New challenges require a new way of thinking - a new paradigm is needed.

We need to be transformed by the renewal of our minds (not our behaviour)! Paul reminded us, "Do not conform to the pattern of this world but be transformed by the renewing of your mind. Then you will be able to test and approve what God's will is —his good, pleasing and perfect will[7]."

 Moses refused to be conformed to the world and understood God's economy, "He considered the reproach of Christ greater wealth than the treasures of Egypt, for he was looking to the reward[8]."

Economics is all about choices, values, resources, and the rules which govern and measure this process. Economics is at the same time both basically simple and highly complex. Economics comes from the

---

6. 2 Corinthians 10:3-5
7. Romans 12:2
8. Hebrews 11:26

Greek word '*oikonomos*', which simply means the management of the household. This cannot be too complicated. '*Oikonomos*' has however changed significantly as modern economics emerged as a function of the modern state and the complexities of the modern financial marketplace.

Former UK prime minister Margaret Thatcher seemed to follow a simple economic model for the nation, considering it as though it were her own housekeeping money. She is famously remembered for telling the European Union that the contribution of the UK was too high. "Give me my money back!" Her view of money was what she learned as a shopkeeper's daughter. Be frugal, spend less than you earn and save for the future. It was about hard work, honesty and living within your means. And it was also about self-improvement, enterprise and enjoying the fruits of your labours (that is, not wanting to see it squandered by government).

Nobel Laureate Joseph Stiglitz made the case for creating a new economic paradigm in a 2010 letter to the Financial Times. "Today, not only is our economy in a shambles," Stiglitz writes, "but so too is the economic paradigm that predominated in the years before the crisis."

Changing paradigms is not easy. Too many have invested too much in the wrong models. Stiglitz says, "Like the Ptolemaic attempts to preserve earth-centric views of the universe, there will be heroic efforts to add complexities and refinements to the standard paradigm. The resulting models will be an improvement and policies based on them may do better, but they too are likely to fail. Nothing less than a paradigm shift will do."

He goes on to note deficiencies in the current economic paradigm and models, and ends the letter with "a new paradigm, I believe, is within our grasp..."

For us, as Christians, it is not a matter of 'thinking up' a new paradigm, but of seeing what God is revealing to us. It is said in the Bible, "Surely the Sovereign Lord does nothing without revealing his plan to his servants the prophets[9]." To believers in exile in Babylon, Jeremiah wrote these encouraging words, "For I know the plans I have for you," declares the Lord, "plans to prosper you and not to harm you, plans to give you hope and a future[10]."

It seems like our world economy will go from crisis to crisis with good years in between. On average, during the past centuries, there has been some sort of crisis every 7-10 years. I remember Rahm Israel Emmanuel, the chief of staff to Obama in 2008, at the start of the economic crisis, saying, "Let's not let a good crisis go to waste. It is an opportunity to do things we have never done before!"

We have excellent opportunities to present the world economy with a new paradigm – that of the economy of the Kingdom of God!

9. Amos 3:7
10. Jeremia 29:11

TWO KINGDOMS

G od has actually two Kingdoms ... both of which belong to Him! The Kingdom of God (or of heaven) which Jesus introduced, ("the Kingdom of God is in the midst of you[1] ...") and the natural Kingdom which God created and which He sustains, also called the common Kingdom.

Running a business and doing ordinary work are activities of the current common kingdom. When Jesus came, he did not establish a state, or the family, or a school, or a business venture. These things already existed and were governed and preserved under the covenant with Noah. The Lord Jesus Christ established one thing, His church, which was to bring in the kingdom of heaven to influence the common kingdom like a stream, like salt in food, like light in darkness, and like leaven in bread.

Abraham Kuyper, a Dutch Reformed theologian started a Christian newspaper, Christian school, a Christian University because he believed that Christ should be pre-eminent in all walks of life. He is famously quoted as saying, "There is not a square inch in the whole domain of human existence over which Christ, who is Sovereign over all, does not cry 'Mine!'"

However, C.S Lewis reminded us that the fallen angel Satan, with his key economic assistant mammon, is active at work breaking up Christian influence in the common kingdom. "There is no neutral ground in the universe; every square inch, every split second, is claimed by God – and counter-claimed by Satan."

The common kingdom is a broken kingdom, but still belongs to God – and He wants it mended!

There's a nice story told about Pope John XIII, when he was still Venice's Cardinal Roncalli. He was having dinner one night with a priestly assistant who was reporting to the cardinal about another priest, a bit of a renegade, who was doing things that were embarrassing the hierarchy. The future pope listened calmly, sipping wine from a goblet. Finally, the assistant cried out in a frustrated tone, "How can you take this so calmly? Don't you realise what this priest is doing?" The cardinal then gently asked the younger priest, "Father, whose goblet is this?" "It is yours, Your Eminence," the priest answered. The cardinal then threw the goblet to the floor, and it shattered into many fragments. "And now whose goblet is it?" he asked. "It is still yours," was the answer. "And so is this priest still my brother in Christ," said the cardinal with a note of sadness in his voice, "even though he is shattered and broken."

God has two kingdoms, the Kingdom of heaven and the Common Kingdom.

The Kingdom Of God...Heaven

This kingdom is a redemptive Kingdom, open only to those who have been redeemed – bought back - called out to serve God and their fellow men according to the gifts and talents given to them.

The citizens of this Kingdom are to live in a strange land, to live a holy life in the midst of many temptations to sin and live a good life among unbelievers so that their good deeds glorify God. They are to participate fully in affairs of the common kingdom. To start businesses, engage in the affairs of ordinary everyday life together with people of all faiths or none, in education, healthcare, governing...

However, as Jesus' parable of the sower tells us, many times our efforts will have varying results, the wheat will grow up with the tares. In this redemptive Kingdom, we receive specific grace … forgiveness, special strength in times of need, guidance, inspiration and wisdom.

The Common Kingdom — A Broken, Rebellious Kingdom

This is the stable or natural order in which we all live irrespective of our God-orientation …. It embraces all cultural activities. Indeed, God honours any activity, which aligns itself with His principles for life and His goals for His Kingdom.

This Common Kingdom, while lasting a long time, is temporary (while earth remains). It was established after the Flood, given to Noah and constituted a Covenant which embraces all people, everywhere.

The covenant for the common kingdom given to Noah and his sons is for them to be fruitful and multiply and fill the earth. It gives both plants and meat for eating and ordains judicial action against such wrongs as murder[2]. This covenant does not talk about any acts of worship, faith or prayer, neither does this covenant indicate any kind of redemption to it to attain life in the world come from obedience. Common grace in this kingdom is available to all. "For he makes his sun rise on the evil and on the good and sends rain on the just and on the unjust[3]."

In this kingdom we do not see the Spirit working as a converting or sanctifying agent but rather working to give gifts of wisdom, courage, creativity and insight—another facet of common grace.

This was illustrated in the movie Amadeus (1984). Salieri is totally confused and bitter that he, a morally good person, has so little talent, while Mozart, a morally despicable person, has obviously been

---

2. Genesis 9:1-6
3. Matthew 5:45

blessed with a rare, God-given musical talent.

Salieri perceived this situation as a failure of divine justice; but in fact, his problem was a failure to understand the doctrine of common grace. God gives good gifts of wisdom, talent, beauty, and skill graciously, that is, in completely unmerited ways. He casts them across the human race like seed, in order to enrich, brighten, and preserve the world. Far from being unfair, God's unmerited acts of blessings make life on earth much more bearable than it should be given the pervasive effects of sin on all of his creation.

Living In The Common Kingdom

In Genesis 6 we read how God got really angry with mankind, and how wicked the human race had become. He resolved 'to blot out man whom I have created from the face of the land[4].' God kept his word and destroyed the world with a great flood, wiping out people and animals alike. But even in this dark time Noah found favour in the eyes of the Lord and he was saved along with his family and a pair of every kind of animal aboard the ark.

After the floodwaters receded God made a new covenant with Noah and with every living creature. This covenant establishes what is called the common kingdom. In this covenant God promises that there will be a stable or natural order until the end of the world. All living creatures will live within this order, and the entire human race will engage in a variety of cultural activities. This covenant embraces all people and not just believers. It ensures the preservation of the natural and social order for all mankind.

The covenant given to Noah and his descendants is very different from the covenant given to Abraham and his offspring. The covenant given to Abraham concerns religious faith and worship, rather than cultural activities; it embraces a holy people which is distinguishable from the rest of the human race, and it bestows the benefits of

---

4. Genesis 6:7

salvation upon this holy people, and it is established for ever and ever. The covenant given to Noah for the common kingdom is very different. It is clear that this covenant for the common kingdom is temporary. It will last a long time, while the earth remains, but we know that this common kingdom will be terminated in some way, at the second coming of Jesus Christ.

We are all called to obey the cultural mandate, as given in modified form in Genesis 9, in which God gave all people, believers and unbelievers alike, the commission to be fruitful and multiply and to exercise dominion over the Earth. The goal of this commission is not to provide a way to attain the new creation but to preserve life and the social order until the end of the present world. Under this covenant all people are morally accountable to God on how they conduct their affairs. The terms of this covenant reminders that we should support legitimate social institutions, such as the family and the state, and must work in cooperation with all people.

The church, the body of believers, the Christians, are chosen race, a royal priesthood, a holy nation, people for His own possession[5]. The kingdom of heaven has broken into this world and is totally distinct from this world as Jesus said, "My kingdom is not of this world[6]." Things are very different in this kingdom of heaven.

The Kingdom Of God

In this kingdom marriage problems should not lead to divorce, slaps on the cheek should not provoke a proportionate retaliation, and the presence of an enemy should not inflame hatred. Instead, Jesus explains that His kingdom is about forgiveness, reconciliation and restoration. If someone has something against you, or slaps you on the right cheek, or persecute you, the response should not be to seek justice but to be reconciled to your brother, not resisting the wrongdoer, turning the other cheek, and not hating your enemies

5. 1 Peter 1:9- 11
6. John 18, 36

but loving your enemies.

In establishing his Church, Jesus points people in the common kingdom to an earthly community that is the gateway to the redemptive kingdom of God. This kingdom is not to be found in the socio-political communities of the wider world. Jesus praised the faith of a centurion but did not comment on the fact that he is a professional soldier, a violent occupation. Later the Pharisees tried to trick Jesus about paying taxes to Caesar. Jesus had the perfect opportunity to condemn the state and to say that states should play by the rules of the kingdom of heaven. But Jesus chose to confirm the legitimate authority of the state, in this case the Roman Empire, to levy taxes and to collect them by force[7]. Paul says the same thing about taxes in Romans 13 and also states that the state rightly wields the sword!

How can we sing the Lord's song in a strange land?

This line from BoneyM's song "Rivers of Babylon", echoes psalm 137, which is a lament from Jewish exiles in Babylon.

On three different occasions Peter refers to Christians as sojourners or exiles. One of Peter's chief concerns in his letters is to instruct Christians about how to live in their present world, and he indicates that the new believers will have an experience similar to that of the Babylonian exiles. Christians are not called to live separate lives from unbelievers but live in lands that are not their own, where they live side-by-side with unbelievers and work alongside them just like the Babylonian exiles. They have been radically distinguished from the world by their faith and their worship of the one true God and by their hope of possessing a true homeland in the future. In this world they mingle with unbelievers, sharing many cultural activities in common with them while remaining distinct from them because of

---

7. Matthew 22:15 – 22

their sinfulness. Living as exiles in a foreign land is characterised by spiritual distinctiveness and cultural commonality.

"Peter, an apostle of Jesus Christ, to God's elect, exiles, scattered ..."Since you call on a Father who judges each person's work impartially, live out your time as foreigners here in reverent fear[8]." Peter encourages us to live as foreigners in a strange land, to live a holy life in the midst of many temptations to sin, and live a good life among unbelievers, so that our good deeds glorify God.

"Dear friends, I urge you, as foreigners and exiles, to abstain from sinful desires, which wage war against your soul. Live such good lives among the pagans that, though they accuse you of doing wrong, they may see your good deeds and glorify God on the day he visits us[9]."

Abraham also lived such a life as an exile and a foreigner in a strange land. As a descendant of Noah, he lived under the covenant given to Noah in the common kingdom, but as recipient of God's special promises in the covenant of grace he also participated in God's redemptive kingdom. When reading about Abraham's life in Genesis 12 to 25 we see that he managed to live as a citizen of both kingdoms by remaining radically separate from the world in his religious faith and worship, but simultaneously engaging in a range of cultural activities in common with his pagan culture.

Abraham participated in the military conflicts of the ancient Near East. He participated in his pagan neighbours' commercial life such as buying a plot of land from the Hittites who lived nearby. He engaged in moral disputes with his pagan neighbours and negotiated mutually acceptable resolutions for them, like his encounter with Abimelech[10], in which they reach an agreement on restitution and future relations which were acceptable to both parties.

We also see that Solomon maintained friendly relations with rulers of

---

8. 1 Peter 1:1,17
9. 1 Peter 2:11
10. Genesis 20:8-14

nations that lived outside Israel's borders. At the height of his reign he dealt cordially with Hiram, the kingdom of Tyre[11], and the Queen of Sheba[12]. Solomon acknowledged to Hiram that there is no one among us who know how to cut timber like the Sidonians[13]."

When the children of Israel were banished to Babylon, we read in a letter from Jeremiah how the Israelites were to conduct themselves in that strange and faraway land. This must have come as a great surprise to the Israelites when they were instructed to build houses, plant gardens, get married, and have children, to multiply and not decrease. In other words, they were to live peaceful lives and pursue their ordinary cultural activities in this foreign land. They were also encouraged to "seek the welfare of the city where I have sent you into exile, and pray to the Lord on its behalf, for in its prosperity you will find your prosperity[14]."

These instructions sound like what we would expect of people living under the covenant to know regarding the common kingdom or how Abraham was to live his life as a foreigner in a strange land. The exiles in Babylon were to continue living holy lives and worshipping the one true God while entering into all the normal activities of family and business life during their exile in Babylon.

In the same way, while in Babylon, Daniel and his friends did not live isolated lives, but they participated in education and politics in common with the Babylonians. Babylon was part of the common kingdom established by God under the covenant given to Noah, and therefore believers in the true God could participate in its cultural life. Daniel and his friends never attempted to turn Babylon into anything other than Babylon. And although they were intimately involved in Babylonian public life, they would not compromise their higher allegiance to God or give up hope that they possessed as citizens of the redemptive kingdom.

---

11. 1 Kings 5
12. 1 Kings 10:11-13
13. 1 Kings 5:6
14. Jeremiah 29:7

Therefore, we can say that we are citizens of two kingdoms. The redemptive kingdom of God on the one hand, and the common kingdom on the other hand. Paul did not hesitate to say that he was proud to be a Roman citizen[15], and yet his hope lay fully in the redemptive kingdom of God, when he said in Philippians 3:20 that our citizenship is in heaven.

Common grace

God also shows common grace by revealing knowledge of himself through human culture, for human culture is simply a wise recognition and cultivation of nature. "When a farmer ploughs for planting... when he has levelled the surface... does he not plant wheat in its place, barley in its plot, and spelt in its field? His God instructs him and teaches him the right way... Grain must be ground to make bread... all this also comes from the Lord Almighty, wonderful in counsel and magnificent in wisdom[16]."

This is remarkable. Isaiah tells us that anyone who becomes a skilful farmer or excels in agricultural science is being taught by God. One commentator writes about this text: "What appears as a discovery, (the proper season and conditions for sowing, farm management, rotation of crops, etc.) is actually the Creator opening His book of creation and revealing His truth."

It is important to note that all human culture ultimately follows the same pattern as farming. Every advancement in human learning, every work of art, and every scientific discovery is simply God 'opening His book of creation and revealing His truth' to us. Of course, the vast majority of farmers in the history of the world did not know that God was doing this, but Isaiah says that God was at work.

This is general revelation, or as theologians call it "the doctrine of common grace." All artistic expressions, skilful farming, scientific

15. Acts 16:37,38
16. Isaiah 28:23–29

discoveries, medical and technological advances are expressions of God's grace. An example from Scripture is found in Exodus 31, where we read how Bezalel was "filled with the Spirit of God, with skill, ability, and knowledge in all kinds of crafts to make artistic designs."

Cyrus was a pagan king that God anointed with his Spirit and chose for world leadership[17]. God also prevented another pagan king from falling into sin[18]. This is an indication of how God's Spirit does not only function as a non-saving ennobling force in the world, but also as a non-saving restraining force in the world. This is not the Spirit working as a converting or sanctifying agent but rather working to give wisdom, courage, creativity and insight—another facet of common grace.

God gives good gifts of wisdom, talent, beauty, and skill graciously, that is, in completely unmerited ways. He casts them across the human race like seed, in order to enrich, brighten, and preserve the world. Far from being unfair, God's unmerited acts of blessings make life on earth much more bearable than it should be given the pervasive effects of sin on all of his creation.

God honours all human activity which aligns itself with his principles for life and his goals for his kingdom. This means that being a Christian is only a relative value with regard to our work in the common kingdom. If any person acts according to the values of the kingdom of God, they will produce a measure of good results whether they are believers or not.

For example, God will honour the investment made in teaching our children to have a sound character whether they are Christian or not. Good business is good business, and this is another example of doing business on the common world in a way which is in alignment with the values of the kingdom of God.

---

17. Isaiah 45:1
18. Genesis 20:6ff

How are we then to live?

On several occasions, the old Testament encourages God's people to pursue their cultural activities with joy and satisfaction. The book of Ecclesiastes offers some good examples. "There is nothing better for a person than that he should eat and drink and find enjoyment in his toil. This also I saw is from the hand of God[19]." "Go, eat your bread, enjoy and drink your wine with a merry heart, for God has already approved what you do. Let your garments be always white. Let not oil be lacking on your head. Enjoy life with the wife whom you love, all the days of your vain life that he has given you under the sun, because that is your portion in life and in your toil at which you toil under the sun[20]."

So how then are we to live?

Firstly, Christians should pursue their worldly activities not with any sense of superiority or triumph over their neighbours but with the spirit of love and service towards them. We have been justified in Christ in order that we may love and serve our neighbour, for this is the fulfilment of the law[21]. The new Testament constantly calls us to gentleness, meekness, patience, and humility[22].

Secondly, we are called to critically engage with human culture. While we seek to treat all people with love and in generosity, we must remain awake and perceptive to the many ways in which sin has corrupted human culture in this fallen world. Paul stated, "We destroy arguments and every lofty opinion raised against the knowledge of God and take every thought captive to obey Christ[23]." Paul acknowledged that living in the common kingdom means that, "We are engaged in spiritual warfare for though we walk in

---

19. Ecclesiastes 2:24
20. Ecclesiastes 9:7-9
21. Romans 13:8 – 10
22. Galatians 5:22-23
23. 2 Corinthians 10:5.

the flesh, we are not waging war according to the flesh. "For the weapons of our warfare are not of the flesh but have divine power to destroy strongholds[24]." We need to realise that the ethic in the common kingdom is rebellious to the things of God, and to be on our guard against the philosophy and empty deceit that seeks to take us captive[25].

Third, we are called to engage in worldly activities with a deep sense of detachment from this world and realise that are true home and to hope is in the world to come. We are encouraged to seek the things that are above not on the earth because our life is hidden in Christ[26]. We are to seek not to lay up treasures of the Earth but to lay up treasures in heaven[27]. We must realise that one day this common kingdom will pass away and we must not seek success and glory in this present age but instead seek to please God, – to renounce ungodliness and worldly passions, and to live self-controlled, and godly lives in this present age, waiting for our blessed hope, the appearing of the glory of our great God and saviour Jesus Christ.

Daniel diligently served his neighbours, maintaining a critical eye, refusing to participate in Babylonian customs that violated God's law, and most of all longing to return to Jerusalem at the end of his exile.

Righteousness, joy and peace

Paul gave a very short description of the economy of the Kingdom when he wrote to Christians in Rome, living in a very different economy. "For the kingdom of God is not a matter of eating and drinking, but of righteousness, peace and joy in the Holy Spirit, because anyone who serves Christ in this way is pleasing to God and

---

24. 2 Corinthians 10:3 – 4
25. Colossians 2:8
26. Colossians 3:3
27. Matthew 6:20.

receives human approval[28]."

Eating and drinking are matters for the common kingdom. The fruits of the kingdom of God, produced by the life given by the holy spirit, in service to Christ, are righteousness, peace and joy. Righteousness has everything to do with accountability, realising that in the final analysis we are responsible to God for how we conduct our business. It is about doing things right, about conformity to a known standard, about conducting affairs honestly and legally.

Peace in the Bible describes the harmony in personal relationships which transcends the experience of the common kingdom. This peace, this 'shalom', is independent of our circumstances, keeping our heads cool while all around us people are losing theirs. Joy is a state of happiness, satisfaction or a contentment in a world which often is frustrating and full of disappointment. It carries the idea of having enough and being in a position to be able to share with others.

Not the externals, but the eternals must be first in our lives: righteousness, peace, and joy. Where do they come from? The Holy Spirit of God at work in our lives.

---

28. Romans 14,17,18.

GOD'S ECONOMY VS THE WORLD ECONOMY

5

The economy of the common kingdom and God's economy are very different. A Biblical description of this contrast is strikingly seen between the first manifestation of God's economy in the newly formed Church in Jerusalem. "And all who believed were together and had all things in common. And they were selling their possessions and belongings and distributing the proceeds to all, as any had need."[1]

Contrast this with Paul's description of the trend in the economy of the common kingdom in his times, which is just like it is in our current times. "But mark this: There will be terrible times in the last days. People will be lovers of themselves, lovers of money, boastful, proud, abusive, disobedient to their parents, ungrateful, unholy, without love, unforgiving, slanderous, without self-control, brutal, not lovers of the good, treacherous, rash, conceited, lovers of pleasure rather than lovers of God— having a form of godliness but denying its power[2]."

As Jesus, from his citizenship of the Kingdom of heaven, said to Pilate, in his citizenship as a Roman; "My kingdom is not of this world ..." The two have conflicting philosophies – not socialism vs capitalism, or any other -ism, but a battle in the heavenly realm. Man's economy has its own set of gurus, its own idols and set of

---

1. 55 Acts 2:43,44
2. 2 Timothy 3:1-5

beliefs! God's economy has Jesus as our supreme teacher, no idols but the Lord God and a set of beliefs as described in the Bible.

Connecting the two

These two economies are, however, not totally separated from one another. In his very first message, Jesus proclaimed, the kingdom of heaven is near. Each time He spoke about the kingdom of heaven, the images which the people saw in their mind were images of flying banners, powerful armies, the gold and ivory of Solomon's day, the nation of Israel restored. It became clear that Jesus was talking about a strangely different kind of kingdom.

The Jews wanted what people have always wanted from a visible kingdom: an economy with a chicken in every pot, full employment, safety from invaders. Jesus announced the His kingdom, which meant dying to self, taking up your cross, renouncing wealth, even loving your enemies. The crowd's expectations crumbled.

Jesus never offered a clear definition of (the economy of -) the kingdom; instead he imparted his vision of it indirectly through a series of stories. His choice of illustrations uses normal everyday activities. It includes men farming and fishing, women baking bread and merchants buying pearls. The Kingdom comes with irresistible power. It is humble and unobtrusive and surprisingly exists together with evil. It is like a farmer going out to sow his seed, some fall among rocks, some get eaten by birds, some get crowded out by weeds.

The mustard seed is so tiny it can fall to the ground and lie unnoticed by human beings and birds alike. Against all odds, God's kingdom will grow and spread throughout the world, bringing shade to the sick, the poor, the imprisoned, the unloved. Why is the kingdom of heaven able to multiply its influence where tradition and religion cannot?

The economy of the kingdom of heaven is like a businessman who specialises in precious jewels. One day he finds a pearl gorgeous enough to make princesses drool with envy. Recognising its value, he liquidates his entire business in order to buy it. Although the purchase costs everything he owns, he does not regret it for a minute. He happily makes the deal as the crowning achievement of his life. His treasure will outlive him, enduring long after his family name has disappeared. His sacrifice – deny yourself, take up your cross – turns out to be a shrewd investment, its outcome not remorse but joy beyond all telling.

As I review the parables about the kingdom of heaven, I realise that the economy of the kingdom of God influences the world in a way which begins very small but will have great effect. It is not an economy which will impose itself on the economy of the common kingdom, forcing any transformation, but an economy which will exercise beneficial service to the good of all who come into contact with it.

Dominion, control and power belong to the Lord. It is clear that He desires to be intimately involved in the affairs of the nations. He has not left the common kingdom to its own ends. I believe that His method of ruling the nations is to make His Church strong and influential, so that its members, through their work and service, give people in the common kingdom an uncommon view of the kingdom of God.

How we as citizens of the kingdom of God live and act in the common kingdom, will determine how the nations can learn from God himself. Our presence as exiles in a foreign kingdom, gives people in the common kingdom a unique learning opportunity as a spiritual portal to the kingdom of God. "When the earth experiences your judgements, the inhabitants of the world learn righteousness[3]."

So, the kingdom of God is a bridge into eternity. It is also a bridge to the common kingdom in our world today. As the kingdom of God is injected into present reality, it is building a bridge into the future and presents a foretaste of what eternity is really like. It is truly a salt that both preserves and seasons this current world with

---

3. Isaiah 26:9

eternity's flavours. It is truly an extension of the light that provides clarity of action and the illumination of the hearts of people and the values of organisations. When the church withholds salt and light from people, organisations, or national structures and policies, it is failing to act as the present world's immune system, designed to keep it as healthy as possible for the sake of God's purposes.

Shrewd

We can see the connection between the two kingdoms, the common kingdom and the kingdom of God, when Jesus is sending out the 12 disciples. "I am sending you out like sheep among wolves. Therefore, be as shrewd as snakes and as innocent as doves. Be on your guard; you will be handed over to the local councils and be flogged in the synagogues. On my account you will be brought before governors and kings as witnesses to them and to the Gentiles[4]." This kind of innocent shrewdness is necessary as we are sent out into the common kingdom, often into a hostile environment. I remember a sign above a bar in an Irish pub. 'We trust in the Lord. All others pay cash!'

Being in the marketplace as a Christian can be very confusing as the workforce is a combination of sheep and wolves, and some of the sheep wear wolves clothing and some of the wolves wear sheep's clothing. Our marketing education and most sales training courses train us to be wolves. God is not calling us to become nicer wolves or even Christian wolves! As Christians, we are to act as sheep following the Great Shepherd and not follow the ways of the world system! How can we be shrewd in all our dealings and yet remain innocent and blameless?

Shrewdness means to be careful to look after your own interests, being cautious and wise, showing good, rational judgment. It is quite a challenge to find the balance between shrewdness and innocence, but these factors were present in Jesus and He will help us make the right decisions in the tough marketplace. Shrewdness means

---

4. Matthew 10:16-18

astuteness or craftiness in dealings with others, especially in using one's understanding and judgment to one's own advantage. Scripture commends it when it is seen in wise words and actions directed towards a worthy goal but condemns it when it takes the form of cunning and deceitful scheming for sinful and selfish ends.

A Spiritual Battle

To understand that the tension between the principles of the economy of the kingdom of God and that of the common kingdom, we need to understand the spiritual forces which undergirds national ideologies and social systems. "For our struggle is not against flesh and blood, but against rulers, against the powers, against the world forces of this darkness, against the spiritual forces of wickedness in the heavenly places[5]."

The ideologies and spiritual climates we face in our culture are underpinning the economy of the world and are glued in place by rebellious spiritual forces. It is clear from Scripture that Satan and his assigned assistants took firm control over the emerging social and ideological systems of people groups and nations. This has led to a development of thought which is against the knowledge of God and disobedient to the principles of His kingdom.

When considering how to live as citizens of the kingdom of God in the common kingdom of this world, we need to find the spiritual forces which are determining the thought processes of the economies in which we find ourselves. This war is being waged on two levels, an upper level by the fallen powers of Satan, and on the lower level by the fallen thinking of man. We must therefore fight the war for the minds and souls of men on both levels.

"For though we walk in the flesh, we do not bore according to the flesh, for the weapons of warfare are not of the flesh, but divinely powerful for the destruction of fortresses. We are destroying speculations and

---

5. Ephesians 6:12

every lofty thing raised up against the knowledge of God, and we are taking every thought captive to the obedience of Christ[6]."

The apostle John tells us that fallen man is driven by these corrupting forces; the sensual lust of the flesh and eyes; the intellectual pride of life and the drive for power; and the effects of the unseen spiritual forces working against him, which are designed to keep him away from the influences of the kingdom of God. "For everything in the world – the lust of the flesh, the lust of the eyes, and the pride of life – comes not from the Father but from the world[7]."

Our modern economic system is founded on challenging Jesus' assertion that man should not live by bread alone. It has been said that, "Modern man can live quite well by bread alone, as long as he can be distracted by means of entertainment and therapy from asking the tough questions about the meaning of what he does."

Mammon

Jesus made a very strong statement which illustrates the spiritual battle. "No one can serve two masters. Either you will hate the one and love the other, or you will be devoted to the one and despise the other. You cannot serve both God and mammon." I believe that mammon is the fallen spirit behind the world's economy. It is, at root, called rightly 'unrighteous mammon,' and is constantly endeavouring to block any attempt to influence the world economy by the principles of God's economy. We need to choose, every day, where our service lies.

The origin of the original word "*Mammonas*" in Aramaic (the language Jesus spoke) comes from a word with the meaning of "permanent" or "that which one can rely on. It is said that Jesus used a play on words saying, '*m'aman*' or 'my trust,' using the word 'amen' or 'so be it'. American coins carry the words, 'in God we trust'. If only it was

---

6. 2 Corinthians 10 3-5
7. 1 John 2:16

like that!

Jesus stated on two occasions. "you cannot serve both God and mammon[8]." During His famous "Sermon on the Mount," He unmasked this power behind money and gave it a name – mammon. Unfortunately, in a lot of our modern Bible translations, the translators chose to use the word money or wealth and consequently rob us of the force of this statement of Jesus. The original word 'mammon' has been translated away by using the words wealth, or money, instead of 'mammon,' so that we miss the true meaning of what Jesus is warning us about! A trick of mammon to allow him to do his work unnoticed - even in our Bibles!

Mammon is not synonymous with money. God and mammon can never be integrated; but God and money should be! Mammon is the fallen spiritual power behind money, seeking to influence people in the spiritual realm to use money unwisely in the worldly or natural realm. "For our struggle is not against flesh and blood, but against the rulers, against the authorities, against the powers of this dark world and against the spiritual forces of evil in the heavenly realms[9]."

Jesus personifies money and considers it a sort of god, which is diametrically opposed to the one true God. However, neither the Jews nor Gentiles of His day knew a god by this name. In other words, Jesus did not use a pagan god to show that one must choose between the true God and a false god. This personification and deification of money also means that it is something that claims divinity. What Jesus is revealing is that money is a power. This term is not to be understood as merely a 'force,' but a 'power' in the specific sense in which it is used in the New Testament.

Mammon, however, is completely opposed to God's economy and wants to thwart God's plans with mankind. Money is his weapon to drive a wedge in relationships between people and between people and God. It is impossible, Jesus said, to serve both. He proposes us a

8. Matthew 6:24 and Luke 16:13
9. Ephesians 6:12

choice; one or the other! There is no way between them. It is about hatred and love; about devotion and contempt, about clinging to one and despising the other. We are dealing with two opposing masters who compete for our dedication and love.

SUITABLE STEWARDSHIP VS PERSONAL PROPERTY 6

The first diversion from the economy of the world is in the area of ownership. A cornerstone of traditional economics is private property. You work for it, you own it, you enjoy it, and you protect it. Holding on to private property can lead to lack of accountability (it's mine!), selfishness, individuality and in the end disillusionment in the power of possessions to bring deep satisfaction and meaning.

Ownership

Property. This is mine. This is yours. Do you think you own anything? You don't.

Ownership is an illusion. So is property. Why? Because all the things you use are only used by you temporarily before they are passed on or thrown away. Be it food, clothing, cars, property, furniture, cell phones, air, water. You never say to anyone 'Don't breathe here! This air is mine!' Of course not. Air is still free, and no one claims to own it. Water is also in a large degree free but is becoming more and more privatised. Food, clothing, cars and land have become utterly privatised. Still, you don't, and never will own anything of it. You use it. You don't own it.

At best, all you can say about ownership is that; 'this is for me to use right now and for as long as I am utilising it.' That is the most 'ownership' there is. Everything that you 'own' is only 'yours' temporarily. It is only borrowed or rented. Your food goes into you and comes out again. So does the water. Even your body is on loan. When you die it goes back into the environment. Ownership is an illusion. Still, it's an illusion we have bought into, but it is no more than an agreement that says, that's ok, we will have a system here that gives some the right to claim vast resources of the planet for themselves, while others get nothing.'

Some of us can say, 'I own my own home.' For many, a home is mortgage. Fail to pay each month and ownership is very quickly questioned. Fail to pay council or city rates, or interest on loans and you could soon find your home gone.

There's no ownership in nature. There's only coexistence, with every part fulfilling their task, and every part being fulfilled in doing so. In a moneyless society and resource-based economy this is how we will look at ownership, since this is the only 'ownership' there is and ever will be. Having a paper that says you own something doesn't make it more 'yours' in the big scheme of things. Whatever you 'own' can be lost in the blink of an eye.

Today ownership is almost equal to accessibility. If, however, you didn't own anything, but had access to virtually everything this planet and humanity can offer, you would 'own' more than the richest people on this planet will ever own. This is the most important thing there is to grasp when it comes to concept of non-ownership:

In a resource-based economy everyone will have access to virtually everything on this planet. Today we think that if this was the case, everyone would rush to the same places and go for the same things, because that is what is seemingly happening today. 'Everyone' seems to run after the same things. And sometimes, some things are more popular than others. But we must remember that a lot of this is due to advertising and promotion seeking a certain behaviour among the population fulfilling the profit motive of the capitalistic system.

One example of a good resource system in today's society is the library. Sometimes you have to wait for books to come back, but more often than not, the books you want to borrow are there for you. If the whole world was like the library, you might have to wait a while going to a certain beach or holiday resort if it was full for the time being. But there would be lots and lots of other places to visit in the meantime, just like there would be lots of other interesting books to read while you were waiting for the one you wanted. Maybe you'd find other, even more interesting books to read, and places to visit, in the meantime.

The idea of ownership builds on the notion of scarcity. The thought that there are not enough of places and books for every one of us. Therefore, it is best to hoard as much as we can while we can. If we don't, we risk being without, not having access and having to live a poor life.

Not owning anything could be the best experience humanity has ever had. It would result in the most abundant lifestyle anyone on this planet could ever dream of. Not owning anything is a notion built on the opposite of scarcity. It is a thought that when we share, everyone will have many times more than what we would ever have if we were to own everything we wanted. Some people try to own as much as possible, thinking this will bring the best lifestyle for them, not realising that sharing will bring more to everyone, even them.

We need to break free from the thought of money, property and ownership and open our eyes to the new virtually unlimited possibilities a sharing society and a resource-based economy can offer.

I have experienced this in my time as a missionary, bringing the gospel to business and professional people. You don't become a missionary, working for a Christian movement, expecting to earn lots of money. If you do, you don't have the mental capacity for the job. I left a well-paid job as CEO of a chemical company and my income dropped like a stone into water. However, I was invited to use people's holiday homes all over the world. I travelled extensively, also enjoying sights I could never afford to see. I was given a car to use. Experiencing sharing is a joy, both to the giver and to the receiver!

We are given the unfathomable privilege of managing God's resources. "You gave them charge of everything you made, putting all things under their authority[1]." This is an awesome responsibility not to be taken lightly. The Biblical message is clear. God owns everything and has given us the task of managing and enjoying whatever He entrusts us with. The laws of the land are designed to protect the right to manage, but let us not talk about ownership, but stewardship.

Stewardship

Stewardship is a way of working which encompasses the responsible planning and management of resources. The concepts of stewardship can be applied across a wide range of human activities, such as the environment and nature, economics, health, property, information, theology, gifts and talents.

Stewardship, being a manager of resources, implies accountability which stimulates a more responsible use of the assets under management. Stewardship implies sustainability, which contributes to the effective and durable use of resources.

The English word 'Stewardship' was originally made up of the tasks of a domestic steward, from stiġ (*house, hall*) and weard, (*ward, guard, guardian, keeper*). Stewardship in the beginning referred to the household servant's duties for bringing food and drink to the castle's dining hall. Stewardship responsibilities were eventually expanded to include everything the domestic, service and management needs of the entire household.

The word that is translated "stewardship" in the Bible is the Greek word *oikonomia*, from which we get our word *economy*. It is two distinct words joined together to create a new word: *oikos*, which comes from the Greek word for *house*, and *nomos*, the Greek word for *law*. The word that is translated "stewardship" literally means "house law" or "house rule."

---

1. Psalm 8:6

We can identify four major principles governing stewardship.

    1.   The principle of ownership.

The concept of stewardship begins with creation. Creation is celebrated not only in Genesis but throughout Scripture, especially in the Psalms, where God's ownership of the universe is declared: "The earth is the Lord's, and all its fullness, the world and those who dwell therein[2]."

God is the author of all things, the Creator of all things, and the owner of all things. Whatever God makes, He owns.

> A.W. Tozer describes the problem of ownership as a 'monstrous substitution.' "There is within the human heart, a tough, fibrous root of fallen life whose nature is to possess, always to possess. It covets things with a deep and fierce passion. Things have become necessary to us, a development never originally intended. God's gifts now take the place of God, and the whole course of nature is upset by this monstrous substitution."

What we own, we own as stewards who have been given gifts from God Himself. God has the ultimate ownership of all of our "possessions." He has loaned these things to us and expects us to manage them in a way that will honour and glorify Him. In the beginning of Genesis, God creates everything and puts Adam in the Garden to work it and to take care of it. It is clear that man was created to work, and that work is the stewardship of all of the creation that God has given him.

This is the fundamental principle of biblical stewardship. God owns everything, we are simply managers or administrators acting on his behalf.

Therefore, stewardship expresses our obedience regarding the administration of everything God has placed under our control,

---

2. Psalm 24:1

which is all encompassing. Stewardship is the commitment of one's self and possessions to God's service, recognising that we do not have the right of control over our property or ourselves.

2. The principle of responsibility.

We have to be responsible for what we actually do with the resources we have been entrusted with. Instead of holding fast to our rights, we are to hold fast to our responsibilities. We are called as God's stewards to manage that which belongs to God. While God has graciously entrusted us with the care, development, and enjoyment of everything he owns as His stewards, we are responsible to manage his holdings well, and according to his desires and purposes. To act responsibly implies we have to be 'response-able,' that is, always ready to give an account of what we have done with the resources.

3. The principle of accountability.

One day each one of us will be called to give an account for how we have managed what the Master has given us.

This is taught by the Parable of the Talents. God has entrusted authority over the creation to us and we are not allowed to rule over it as we see fit. We are called to exercise our dominion under the watchful eye of the Creator managing his creation in accord with the principles He has established.

Like the servants in the Parable of the Talents, we will be called to give an account of how we have administered everything we have been given, including our time, money, abilities, information, wisdom, relationships, and authority.

We will all give account to the rightful Owner as to how well we managed the things He has entrusted to us.

4. The principle of reward.

Paul writes, "Whatever you do, work at it with all your heart, as working for the Lord, not for men, since you know that you will receive an inheritance from the Lord as a reward. It is the Lord Christ you are serving[3]."

The Bible shows us in the parables of the Kingdom that faithful stewards who do the master's will with the master's resources can expect to be rewarded incompletely in this life, but fully in the next. We all should long to hear the master say what he exclaims, "Well done, good and faithful servant! You have been faithful with a few things; I will put you in charge of many things. Come and share your master's happiness[4]!" When asked, "What would you like to hear when you come to stand before Jesus?" The most-often heard reply is "Well done, good and faithful servant." Our life-long quest must be to please Jesus.

Jesus commands, "Do not lay up for yourselves treasures on earth, where moth and rust destroy and where thieves break in and steal but lay up for yourselves treasures in heaven[5]." These treasures are the rewards for faithful stewardship.

We need to embrace this larger biblical view of stewardship, which connects everything we do with what God is doing in the world.

We need to be faithful stewards of all God has given us within the opportunities presented through his providence to glorify Him, serve the common good and further his Kingdom.

Manager of Gods resources

Paul states that "You are bought and paid for, therefore glorify God with your body[6]."

---

3. Colossians 3:23,24
4. Matthew 25:21
5. Mathew 6:19,20a
6. 1 Corinthians 6:23

Therefore, everything that I have, belongs to God and I am to deploy all my assets to honour God, to use for His purposes. This is a great antidote for selfishness and forms the basis for generosity.

You are not your own, you were bought with a price. This price was, of course, the precious blood of our Saviour who gave His life for us. We have been bought back, which the Bible calls 'redemption.' We have been redeemed, bought out of slavery to the world's system and brought into the economy of the Kingdom. At the cross of Christ, all the powers of the world were present, waiting for the death of Christ, to put an end to His power and influence, so that they could continue ruling.

There was military power, in the form of the Roman soldiers. There was political power in the form of the Roman governor, Pontius Pilate. There was religious power in the form of the Pharisees. There was also financial power in the form of Judas, who was selling Jesus for thirty pieces of silver to the Pharisees. Jesus, through His death and resurrection broke all these powers, so that all who believe in Him and accept His provision, can be set free from these powers.

By allowing Himself, once and for all, to be subject to the economy of the world, Jesus could set us free from this economy and bring us into the economy of the Kingdom. This means everything we are and have, has been transferred from one economy into another.

Remember the illustration of the Gulf Stream? Still in the ocean, but distinct from it, still in the sea, but a strong current has started, a new movement has begun. In this way, a dynamic new cooperation has started in which God has a part to play and I have a part to play.

He is Owner, I am His manager. That means He bears responsibility for providing, leading and evaluating our performance. My responsibilities are to find out what the Owner requires, to carry out His priorities and to work to realise His goals.

A steward's primary goal is to be "found faithful" by his master[7]. He proves himself faithful by wisely using the master's resources to accomplish the tasks delegated to him. Those resources include not only money but time, gifting, relationships, employment and life opportunities.

Randy Alcorn said, "Seen from this perspective, stewardship isn't a narrow subcategory of the Christian life. On the contrary, stewardship is the Christian life." It aligns with a similar quote by John Piper, "The issue of money and lifestyle is not a side issue in the Bible. The credibility of Christ in the world hangs on it."

The Foundation of the Kingdom Economy

When nations on earth refuse to recognise God as the Creator, their governments assume ownership of that which God has created. The Kingdom of God, on the other hand, recognises God as the Creator, and so its government recognises His ownership of all that He has created.

This is perhaps the most fundamental truth of the universe—stated in the very first words of the Bible, "*In the beginning God created the heavens and the earth*[8]." Any law, rule or principle that does not proceed from this truth is flawed.

When God divided up the land of Canaan for the families of each tribe, He removed from most of the land its speculative value. He did this by telling them that they had no right to buy and sell land, except houses which were built in urban areas. "The land, moreover, shall not be sold permanently, for the land is Mine; for you are but aliens and sojourners with Me. Thus, for every piece of property, you are to provide for the redemption of the land[9]."

As Creator, God held the absolute right to His created domain. This

---

7. 1 Corinthians 4:2
8. Genesis 1:1
9. Leviticus 25:23,24

meant that the people's privilege of land ownership was conditional upon their obedience to the law of God. The people were but "sojourners" with God. They were living on someone else's land, and so they did not have unlimited freedom to use the land as they pleased. The utilised land must be placed under the direction and authority of God Himself.

The land laws of the Bible are the basic economic laws for a Kingdom nation. Included in God's land ownership is His ownership of all mineral rights - "The silver is Mine, and the gold is Mine, declares the Lord of hosts[10]."

God's ownership is also seen in the law of the tithe. Whenever man derives income from God's work in creation, he must give God a tenth of it for the support of Kingdom government. This includes farming, ranching, mining, fishing, and lumbering. The tithe is not based upon one's own labour, but upon God's desire to see a return on His own labour. The tithe is also an important recognition of God as the Creator and Owner of all that He has created.

God owns the land, and man is His steward. While we may talk of our personal ownership of land, we must keep in mind that we mean *ownership under God*. Our ownership is limited by God's rights.

In this way, we need have no problem with conforming to the apostle Peter's instructions to, "be subject for the Lord's sake to every human institution, whether it be to the emperor as supreme, or to governors[11] ..." We need also have no problems with to paying our taxes and obeying Jesus' command to "render to Caesar the things that are Caesar's."[12]

When you realise that all of life, including all of Caesar's rights and power and possessions belong to God, then you will be in a proper frame of mind to render to Caesar what is Caesar's.

---

10. Haggai 2:8
11. 1 Peter 2:13
12. 75. Matthew 22:21

When you know that all is God's, then anything you render to Caesar you will render for God's sake. Any authority you ascribe to Caesar you will ascribe to him for the sake of God's greater authority. Any obedience you render to Caesar you will render for the sake of the obedience you owe first to God. Any claim Caesar makes on you, you test by the infinitely higher claim God has on you.

What is Caesar's is determined by the fact that everything is God's first, and only becomes Caesar's by God's permission and design.

Only God decides what is a rightful, limited rendering to Caesar. The only reason God ordains the rights of a Caesar is for His own sake.

Jesus and Peter are calling for Christians to have the mindset of an alien and a citizen at the same time. "Live as free people, not using your freedom as a cloak of evil, but being servants of God[13]." We are God's servants, not the servants of any government. We are free from all governments and human institutions, because we belong to the owner of the universe and share in that inheritance ("fellow heirs with Christ"). God has made us and bought us for himself. Being freed from the world and from Caesar, God sends us for a season back into the foreign structures and institutions of society to 'be faithful in that which is another's.' We are to live out the alien ideas of another kingdom in the midst of our earthly homeland.

There will always be tension as we live in these two kingdoms. But God sends us in, not out, and calls us to influence the world's economy by practicing stewardship faithfully.

Back to the Gold Standard!

In 1717, as 'Master of the Mint', Isaac Newton fixed the price of one ounce of gold at £3 17s 10 ½ d. This Gold Standard dominated economics for over 200 years. The value of paper money was fixed to this standard. Britain abandoned the standard after the depression in 1931 and its last remains were interred in 1971 by President Nixon.

---

13. 1 Peter 2:16

Our day-to-day use of money is decoupled from anything which has intrinsic worth. Money is worth only promises!

Christians should get back on the spiritual "Gold Standard"! There is something of intrinsic and eternal worth which measures everything we think, feel and do about money. It is a rich, timeless biblical perspective on money that measures and tests our spending and saving, giving and borrowing, our financial planning and our lifestyle.

This standard is defined by God's ownership of everything we have. When thinking about spending, we ask "how should I spend God's money?' Instead of asking 'how much of my income should I give to God?', I should ask 'how much of Gods money should I keep for myself?' Instead of lending money for a need, we should be thinking, 'can I better give the money in order not to burden the one in need?'

God's goals are our ultimate standard.

Back to the gold standard means … acknowledging that God owns everything, that I am His steward called to manage His property faithfully and that money should be used for relational purposes, first to love God then to love people.

"You must love the Lord your God with all your heart, all your soul, and all your mind.' 38 This is the first and greatest commandment. A second is equally important: 'Love your neighbour as yourself.'." (Matthew 22:37–39)

In the Bible gold is a symbol of love. And not just any old love. Gold symbolizes higher loves than, say, love of food and drink or love of fresh air and sunshine—as good and wholesome as those loves are. As the most precious metal known in Bible times, gold represents the most precious kind of love.

From a spiritual perspective, gold, in the Bible, represents heavenly and spiritual love, which is the love of God and the love of our fellow human beings. These are the loves that Jesus tells us are central to human life. Now, this love is not just a theoretical thing that we feel in our heart. If we truly love God and our fellow human beings, we will spend our lives doing good things for them. And even though we cannot do good things for God directly, Jesus tells us that if we do good things for other people, we are doing good things for God. "Truly, I say to you, as you did it to one of the least of these my brothers, you did it to me[14]."

So gold is not only a symbol of our love for God and our fellow human beings, it is also a symbol of all the good and thoughtful things we do for them out of love. The Bible says that the streets of the heavenly city, new Jerusalem, are paved with pure gold[15], meaning that the streets of the city are paved with pure love—meaning that in God's kingdom the roads we travel every day are pathways of love.

---

14. Matthew 25:34-40
15. Revelation 21:21

HOLY SPIRIT VS MAMMON

The invisible hand

The invisible hand is a term coined by economist Adam Smith in his 1776 book "An Inquiry into the Nature and Causes of the Wealth of Nations".

In his book he states: "Every individual necessarily labours to render the annual revenue of the society as great as he can. He generally neither intends to promote the public interest, nor knows how much he is promoting it ... He intends only his own gain, and he is in this, as in many other cases, led by an invisible hand to promote an end which was no part of his intention. Nor is it always the worse for society that it was no part of his intention. By pursuing his own interest he frequently promotes that of the society more effectually than when he really intends to promote it. I have never known much good done by those who affected to trade for the public good."

At a forum in Washington, Cardinal Óscar Rodríguez Maradiaga of Honduras, said that the world financial system "has been built as a new idolatry." During his keynote address, Cardinal Rodríguez issued a ringing endorsement of the church's competency to critique economic systems. "Some of the church's critics ask: 'What is the hierarchy of the church doing in the economy? They know nothing about the economy.' The church knows about the economy because we know about the human being. The human being was not made for the economy, but the economy was made for the human being."

He added that, "The market's invisible hand has become a thief."

It seems like the market's 'invisible hand' has become a thief. Where is this supposed invisible hand gone? Did it ever exist?

What has happened to our free market system in which this hand seems to have disappeared? What happened to the economists and politicians in Greece some years ago when 'cooking the books' in order to get into the eurozone? What happened to our bankers who used our money to speculate using systems they didn't understand and lose not only our money but our trust? What happened to our major corporations who use people in order to improve share prices?

Supposedly, this invisible hand will miraculously turn business which is based on self-interest into some public good. In 2009, Lloyd C. Blankfein, the chief executive of the large bank Goldman Sachs, which has attracted widespread media attention over the size of its staff bonuses, and was accused of playing huge role in the crisis which began in 20008, says he believes banks serve a social purpose and are "doing God's work."

"We're very important," Blankfein said in an interview with The Times of London. "We help companies to grow by helping them to raise capital. Companies that grow create wealth. This, in turn, allows people to have jobs that create more growth and more wealth. It's a virtuous cycle." His envisaged 'trickle down' effect is not happening in an economy where the rich get richer and the poor get poorer. We are still experiencing an ever-widening gap in wealth.

Jim Wallis wrote a great opening to an article in the Sojourners magazine, "Our life together can be better. Ours is a shallow and selfish age, and we are in need of conversion—from looking out just for ourselves to also looking out for one another. It's time to hear and heed a call to a different way of life, to reclaim a very old idea called the common good. Jesus issued that call and announced the kingdom of God—a new order of living in sharp contrast to all the political and religious kingdoms of the world. That better way of life was meant to benefit not only his followers but everybody else too."

The four major pillars on which our current economic system is built are: Free markets; Growth; Debt & Consumption.

1. The 'Free Market' has taken on almost godly attributes and is worshipped all around the globe at the banks and shopping malls – 'temples of mammon' as someone has called them. Capitalists refer to the 'trickle-down' functioning of the market. If it rains on people at the top, the ones underneath get wet. It is plainly obvious that this does not always work that way!

    We are not absolutely free and neither are markets. We are only free to work within certain boundaries which do not violate public good. The Spirit of God asks us to seek our freedom in adhering to His words, which will make us truly free.

2. Growth is the focus of our economic system which goes together with profit maximisation, which leads to unnecessary risks with our assets and manipulation of people. The period 2008-2015 show how flawed this is. We are still balking at the bonuses for managers who failed. God's Spirit asks us to answer the question 'How Much Is Enough,' to be satisfied with that, and give any surplus to those who do not have enough.

3. The third pillar is Debt. National debt has risen to uncontrollable heights, personal debt has enslaved millions! The worst is – it was done deliberately! Private debt is causing millions anxiety, stress and loss of hope. Both nationally and privately, the Bible proverb has been proven true "As the rich rule over the poor, so the borrower becomes slave to the lender[1]!" The Spirit of God sets people free.

4. Consumption is the motor of our economy and partly determines our identity – to paraphrase Descartes,

---

1. Proverbs 22:7

"Consumo ergo sum - I buy, therefore I am." It has become a goal in itself. The Spirit of God promotes sharing, giving and responsible purchasing.

Economist Arnold Harberger said in an interview for a documentary, "…the forces of the market are just that: They are forces; they are like the wind and the tides. If you want to try to ignore them, you ignore them at your peril. If you find a way of ordering your life which harnesses these forces to the benefit of society, that's the way to go." We Christians have the wonderful resource of the power of the Holy Spirit with which to order our lives.

It is only the presence of the Spirit of God on this earth which prevents us all from descending into complete disaster. God never has to punish us. He only has to leave us alone and we can do that job quite nicely. We need to rediscover the role of God's Spirit in turning self-interest into public good. Only God can do that …!

Pope Francis has warned of unbridled capitalism. According to him, this is a "new tyranny. He called on world leaders to fight poverty and growing inequality in the world. In a 2013 document, the first thing he wrote himself since he became Pope, he criticised the 'worship of money,' and calls on rich people to share their money. "How is it possible that it is not news when an elderly homeless person dies, but it is news when the stock index lose two points," the Pope wonders. The Pope is convinced that the world's problems can only be solved by rejecting the full autonomy of the market and speculating with money. He believes that there is no place for an economy of exclusion and inequality. "Such an economy destroys," writes Francis.

So, where is this invisible hand? I believe that this 'invisible hand' is still very much with us, directing the economy of the world and not bringing the results we are looking for. I believe Jesus unmasked this 'invisible hand' when He introduced us to the power behind money, which He called mammon.

There is another invisible hand, which can turn self-interest into seeking the common good, which is to be found in the Spirit of God.

As Jesus said, "When the Spirit of truth comes, he will guide you into all the truth, for he will not speak on his own authority, but whatever he hears he will speak, and he will declare to you the things that are to come." (John 16:13)

Mammon

Jesus calls money mammon, an Aramaic word that usually means "money" and also can mean "wealth." Here Jesus personifies money and considers it a sort of god. However, neither the Jews nor Gentiles of His day knew a god by this name. In other words, Jesus did not use a pagan god to show that one must choose between the true God and a false god. Jesus gives this term a force and a precision that it did not have in its milieu. This personification and deification of money also means that it is something that claims divinity. What Jesus is revealing, is that money is a power.

Power is something that acts by itself. It has spiritual meaning and direction. Power is never neutral. Money as power orients, moves, and controls. This power competes for our allegiance to God. "No servant can serve two masters; for either he will hate the one and love the other, or else he will be loyal to the one and despise the other. You cannot serve God and mammon[2]." Jesus calls for a choice. Who will we serve, God or mammon?

The Bible speaks a lot about the struggle with 'the powers' of this world.' When Paul was in Ephesus, he suffered greatly, not only from the people there, but also spiritually. "For we do not wrestle against flesh and blood, but against the rulers, against the authorities, against the cosmic powers over this present darkness, against the spiritual forces of evil in the heavenly places[3]." Mammon is such a power.

Paul Tillich wrote, "These powers drive nations and individuals into insoluble conflicts, internal and external; into arrogance and insanity,

---

2. Matthew 6:24
3. Ephesians 6:12

into revolt and despair, into inhumanity and self-destruction. Each of us is involved in these conflicts and driven to a greater or lesser degree by these forces. The personal life of each of us is in some way determined by them. No security is guaranteed to anyone; no house, no work, no friend, no family, no country anywhere in the world is safe, no plans are certain of fulfilment, all hopes are threatened. This is not a new state of things in human history. But what is new is that during a few years of comparative safety, we had forgotten that this is the true state of things."

There is clear Biblical and experiential evidence for an invisible world that affects us both positively and negatively. For every visible foreground to a person's life-embracing family, work, community service, leisure, citizenship and church-there is an invisible background that is profoundly influential. We want to do good, to serve God and our neighbour, to do an honest day's work, but we find ourselves confronted with 'the system'-with frozen tradition, with intractable institutions, with deeply engrained social patterns that resist us, and, finally, with the world of spiritual beings and forces. What makes life difficult is systemic evil.

We constantly experience unjust and unloving systems of business and finance, principles of conformity and social patterns, that marginalise the life of faith or positively oppose it. In addition, there is the world of the spirits. All these are interdependently, systemically resistant to God's purposes in the world and hinder the steps of believers. Scripture describes the realities encountered by people in their life in this world by means of various names, among them the world, the flesh, demons, Satan, angels and the divine council. "For I am sure that neither death nor life, nor angels nor rulers, nor things present nor things to come, nor powers, nor height nor depth, nor anything else in all creation, will be able to separate us from the love of God in Christ Jesus our Lord[4]."

The difficulty we have with these powers is that they were created by

---

4. Romans 8:38,39

God to give structure and order to our universe, but they have gone wild and now we have to deal with these fallen social structures. Karl Barth says we experience these as political, financial and juridical forces; traditions, doctrines and practices that regulate religion and life. These are no longer holding society together.

On one hand, they are hard-wired to form structures which are to be beneficial to us all. However, because the powers which govern these are fallen powers, they become tyrannical and misuse the power they have. They give basic structure and form but have an inbuilt tendency to misuse their powers. Of course, not all of the problems in the world economy can be attributed to these fallen powers. People also have an inbuilt propensity to choose the wrong ways of doing things! We should not, however, minimalise the effect of these fallen powers and neglect arming ourselves against them. "Put on the whole armour of God, that you may be able to stand against the schemes of the devil[5]."

We are still to continue using these worldly structures, because God created them for our benefit. We are to permeate these structures with the fruits of the Spirit. Peter wrote, "Be subject for the Lord's sake to every human institution, whether it be to the emperor as supreme, or to governors as sent by him to punish those who do evil and to praise those who do good. For this is the will of God, that by doing good you should put to silence the ignorance of foolish people. Live as people who are free, not using your freedom as a cover-up for evil, but living as servants of God[6]."

So, how do we overcome mammon?

In overcoming mammon, four words seem to me to be essential. Decide, dethrone, desacralise and disarm. Then live in victory by constantly living and working in God's economy.

---

5. Ephesians 6:11
6. 1 Peter 2:13-16

Decide

A decision is needed - serve God or serve mammon. Most Christians have never been faced with such a decision, which I believe is a one-time major life decision, followed by daily obedience and devotion to following Gods ways of handling money. This decision could be likened to baptism. A one-time event followed by daily following Jesus.

The great Reformer, Martin Luther, once wrote that, "There are three conversions necessary: the conversion of the heart, the conversion of the mind, and the conversion of the purse. Of these three, it may well be that we find the conversion of the purse to be the most difficult."

Charles Spurgeon writes, "With some (Christians) the last part of their nature that ever gets sanctified is their wallets."

Dethrone.

Then, we need to dethrone mammon in our lives. Recognising Jesus' victory over mammon at the cross, taking this cross up daily, living out of Jesus' victory will break the power of mammon in our lives, "by cancelling the record of debt that stood against us with its legal demands. This he set aside, nailing it to the cross. He disarmed the rulers and authorities and put them to open shame, by triumphing over them in him[7]." Jesus broke the power of money by allowing himself to be sold as a slave to the world system and to be bought by the Pharisees, thereby breaking this power of buying and selling to set us free!

When we consciously transfer all that we possess into God's hands, and accept His ownership of all things, we take mammon off the throne and take away his leadership and influence over our finances. If you have transferred everything to God, then nothing belongs to mammon and all possessions and money fall under Gods control.

---

7. Colossians 2:14,15

Desacralise

Then, we need to desacralise money by taking away it's sacred, holy powers. Money must never be a goal in itself and become an idol. We desacralise money by giving the first and best part of all income and moving money into God's economy! Then the work of mammon, the spoiler, will be negated.

"Bring the full tithe into the storehouse, that there may be food in my house. And thereby put me to the test, says the Lord of hosts, if I will not open the windows of heaven for you and pour down for you a blessing until there is no more need. I will rebuke the devourer for you, so that it will not destroy the fruits of your soil, and your vine in the field shall not fail to bear, says the Lord of hosts[8]." The 'devourer', mammon, can no longer spoil Gods' plans for us.

We desacralise money by bringing grace into the world of buying and selling. God receives the money which is given and brings it into His economy … and from this storehouse, He will supply.

Give with a glad and generous heart. Giving has a way of routing out the 'tough old miser' within us. Even the poor need to know that they can give. Just the very act of letting go of money, or some other treasure, does something within us. It destroys the demon greed. Giving is winning a victory over the dark powers that seek to control and oppress us. The powers that energise money cannot abide that very unnatural of acts - giving. In the world economy, money is made for taking, for bargaining, for manipulating, but not for giving. This is exactly why giving has such ability to defeat the powers of money.

Disarm

Through our Christian ministry, we can contribute to disarming the powers, returning them to their original purpose.

---

8. Malachi 3:10,11a

We deal with the spirit of the world through conforming to the will of God and learning to discern what is right. "Do not be conformed to this world, but be transformed by the renewal of your mind, that by testing you may discern what is the will of God, what is good and acceptable and perfect[9]. The Lord's part is to transform us from within, so that we can transform, rather than be conformed by our world, as we penetrate it in our work and mission.

We must pray for our businesses, organisations and government institutions. Karl Barth once said that "to clasp the hands in prayer is the beginning of an uprising against the disorder of the world. "Submit yourselves therefore to God. Resist the devil, and he will flee from you. Draw near to God, and He will draw near to you[10]."

We must call people to embrace the reign of Christ through repentance and faith. Our duty is not to bring the powers to our knees: this is Christ's task. Our duty is to arm ourselves with Christ. "He disarmed the rulers and authorities and put them to open shame, by triumphing over them in him[11]."

Christ's complete victory over the principalities and powers, over Satan, sin and death, assures us that there is nowhere in the universe so demonic that a Christian might not be called to serve there. We fight a war that is already won. Therefore, as far as is now possible, Christians should 'christianise' the powers, through involvement in education, government and social action. We need to work to solve problems of pollution, food distribution, injustice, genetic engineering and the proliferation of violence and weaponry, knowing that this work is ministry, cooperating with what Christ wants to do in renewing all creation.

We are to constantly live with the principles of the Kingdom economy in mind. "Set your minds on things that are above, not on things that

---

9. Romans 12:2
10. James 4:7,8
11. Colossians 2:15

are on earth[12]." This involves following God's principles of managing our economic life, instead of being influenced by mammon. We need to depart from a lifestyle which is centred on money and possessions and practice a lifestyle of simplicity. A good starting point is to answer the question for yourself, "How much is enough?" How much is enough for your current responsibilities, in the economic strata God has called you to?

Another invisible hand

I believe the Holy Spirit is another 'invisible hand' by which God directs all things — both animate and inanimate, seen and unseen, good and evil — toward a worthy purpose, which means His will must finally prevail. As the psalmist said, "His kingdom rules over all[13]." God is running the universe today, even though there are some who think that it has slipped out from under Him.

There are three properties we need to keep in mind before we can properly understand this 'invisible hand' of God in relationship to the material universe and to man in particular.

First, is the hand of creation. We understand by "creation" that God spoke this universe into existence. He has not abandoned His creation but is waiting patiently for the fulfilment of His creation. "For the creation waits with eager longing for the revealing of the sons of God. For the creation was subjected to futility, not willingly, but because of him who subjected it, in hope that the creation itself will be set free from its bondage to corruption and obtain the freedom of the glory of the children of God[14]." We can be intimately involved in co-creating with God as we seek to bring peace, justice and righteousness into the world's economy.

Second, is the hand of preservation. It is by God's preservation that the universe is held together. "And He is before all things, and by

---

12. Colossians 3:2
13. Psalm 103:19
14. Romans 8:19-21

Him all things consist[15]." We have a universe that runs like clockwork today, run by the Lord Jesus Christ. "He upholds the universe by the word of His power. Jesus has the last word. He will not allow anything to happen which is not, ultimately, for our good.

Third, is the hand of providence. Providence is the way that God is directing the universe. He is moving it into tomorrow — He is moving it into the future by His providence. Providence means "to provide." God will provide. Providence means that the hand of God is in the glove of human events. When God is not at the steering wheel, He is the backseat driver. He is the coach who calls the signals from the bench. Providence is the unseen rudder on the ship of state. God is the pilot at the wheel during the night watch. The hand of God is very active in directing the affairs of our world!

---

15. Colossians 3:17

BUILD WITH ASSETS, NOT DEBT

The origins of debt go all the way back to the fall of man in the Garden of Eden. When Eve was tempted by the serpent and had to give an account of what she had done, she explained, *"the serpent deceived me ... then I ate[1]."* This word 'deceived' in Hebrew comes from a root 'nasha' which represents a homonym = a word having different meanings - to deceive, and also to lend at interest.

This Hebrew word is strongly linked to the Hebrew word 'nashak' which means 'to strike with a sting!' This appears for instance in Habakkuk 2:7. "Will not your creditors (nashak) suddenly arise? Will they not wake up and make you tremble? Then you will become their victim."

This tells us that lending at interest is at its root a deceit, tempting people into bondage. Just like the serpent tempted Eve into a bargain of debt which she could never, ever repay. Borrowing money is almost like opening a Pandora's Box, because we never know what is going to happen next! Opening Pandora's Box refers to getting into a situation over which one has very little control.

According to the old Greek story Pandora was to be the first of a race of women, the first bride and a great misery, who would live with mortal men as companions only in times of plenty, and desert

---

1. Genesis 3:13

them when times became difficult! (Does this sound like a bank?) The first woman, Pandora, was sent as a curse to Zeus' men and was given a present upon her marriage. The present was a box that she was told never to open. Needless to say her curiosity got the better of her (like eating forbidden fruit) and she unleashed eight demons unto the world. The first seven being the seven deadly sins, and the last, which she managed to capture, was hope.

The Czech professor, Dr. Tomas Sedlacek said at a conference I helped organise in Berlin, "Eve and Adam grab the opportunity and eat the fruit. The original sin has the character of excessive, unnecessary consumption. It is not of a sexual nature. A desire for something she doesn't need is awakened in Eve. The living conditions in paradise were complete, and yet everything God had given the two wasn't enough. In this sense, greed isn't just at the birthplace of theoretical economics, but also at the beginning of our history. Greed is the beginning of everything."

Prof. Jacques Ellul, wrote in his wonderful book 'Money & Power,' "The Hebrew word for money,' *kesef*, comes from a verb meaning 'to desire, to languish after something.' This implies, that from the beginning, when the Hebrew language was being formed, the spiritual character of money as well as its power was already stressed. This relation between money and desire shows that lust for money dwells in us."

Practical problems with debt

There are a number of practical problems associated with debt.

1. Debt encourages you to spend more than you can afford.

There's something about debt that tempts you to keep spending even when you can't afford the payments. Part of the allure of debt is the fact that you can get the emotional high from getting new things now, without having to deal with the pain of parting with the money now. It can almost feel like you're getting something for nothing. But eventually, that spending will catch up with you, and it won't feel so good then.

2.   Debt costs money

Debt feels to set you free when you're swiping your card or signing loan documents, but it's not freedom at all. In general, you pay a price for the debt you create. That price comes in the form of interest. The higher the interest rate, the more you'll end up paying for your debt. Also, the longer it takes you to pay off and the higher your debt load, the more interest you'll pay. When consolidating loans, a short-term relief may be gained, but you'll end up paying much more in the long term.

3.   Debt borrows from future income

Anytime you take out a loan or charge something on your credit card; you're borrowing from the money you hope to earn in the future. Do you want to spend your money paying for something you've already used up and don't get much value from anymore?

4.   Debt can keep you from reaching your financial goals

Monthly debt payments limit the amount of money you have to spend on other things, not just retirement, but the trip you always wanted to take or giving generously. The more debt you accumulate, the more your monthly payments will be, and the less you have to spend on everything else.

Credit card, car, and student loan debt are all considered when applying for a home loan. If your other debt payments are too high, you may get turned down for a mortgage loan. That means you'll be stuck renting, or on your current mortgage until you pay off some of your other debt.

5.   Debt can lead to stress and serious medical problems.

When you have debt, it's hard not to worry about how you're going to make your payments or how you'll stay away from taking on more debt to make ends meet. The stress from debt can lead to mild to severe health problems including ulcers, migraines, depression, and even heart attacks.

6.   Debt can hurt relationships

Debt puts unnecessary pressure on the household's finances and creates a lack of financial security for your spouse and your children. Debt can spark arguments about who is creating debt, how much debt is too much, and who's responsible for the debt that's accumulated. These fights can escalate and lead to a breakdown in the marriage.

Unpaid loans can seriously damage relationships with friends.

Spiritual problems with debt

God wants us to love and honour others by paying what is due, fully, and on time! "Pay to all what is owed to them: taxes to whom taxes are owed, revenue to whom revenue is owed, respect to whom respect is owed, honour to whom honour is owed. Owe no one anything, except to love each other, for the one who loves another has fulfilled the law.[2]" When a debt I not paid back, fully and timely, relationships start to get tense, and even break up. Then we cannot love our neighbour as we ought to. I remember being in church one day and I witnessed a friend giving someone else an envelope with some money - a loan, I learned later. After handing over the money, he gave the other person a big hug. I asked, 'why are you giving him a big hug?' 'Well,' he answered, 'that's probably the last time I'll ever see him.' Those who have outstanding loans due to them will understand the changes in your feelings towards those who owe you money.

The Bible explains that the main problem with debt is that it takes away your freedom. Solomon stated that when you borrow, you place yourself under someone else's authority, who has first call on your money (after the government.) "The rich rules over the poor, and the borrower is the slave of the lender[3]." In addition, Paul explains that

---

2. Romans 13:8
3. Proverbs 22:7

although it may be ok to borrow, we must be careful not to allow ourselves to be controlled by it. "All things are lawful for me," but not all things are helpful. "All things are lawful for me," but I will not be dominated by anything[4]."

David in a psalm refers to those who borrow and do not repay as 'wicked,' or 'hostile' to God[5]. I believe that we run the risk of God pulling back from our affairs when we do not pay bills on time. He lives in us and He will not allow Himself to become party to wickedness! Paying back our commitments will make sure that our relationship with God remains true. When we break our promise we are involving God, who always keeps His word – we should too! "God is not man, that he should lie, or a son of man, that he should change his mind. Has he said, and will he not do it? Or has he spoken, and will he not fulfil it[6]?"

Debt is actually a bookkeeping term, but is also a moral term. Technically, you are indebted when taking out any loan. Having a loan is not sinful. Morally and spiritually, you are not in debt if you keep all your promises completely and on time. We become morally and spiritually indebted when you do not have any assets, which you can immediately sell or realise, to cover the debt and when promises to pay are not kept. This is deceit.

You are also in debt, spiritually, when it causes anxiety. "And the effect of righteousness will be peace, and the result of righteousness, quietness and trust forever[7]." Anxiety is a sign of unrighteousness. A sign of doing things right is peace.

The underlying problem

Since the Second World War, my post-war generation has enjoyed wonderful economic growth. Who could imagine today, that in the

---

4. 1 Corinthians 6:12
5. Psalm 37:21
6. Numbers 23:19
7. Isaiah 32:17

fifties and sixties a car was an absolute luxury and a holiday abroad was reserved for high incomes? That many people had no telephone, or indeed a TV! Today, these are commonplace.

We have difficulty imagining a real crisis.

As I write this, it is almost twelve years since the 2008 crash. This was the greatest jolt to the global financial system in almost a century – it pushed the world's banking system towards the edge of collapse. Unfortunately, no lessons were learned, it is business as usual again and the crisis has been relegated to a blip in the past.

The 2008-2015 crisis was caused, on the surface, by over-excessive borrowing to finance risky spending. Under the surface, forming the underlying shifting sands, was a phenomenon we don't like to talk about - greed. The late sixties and seventies of the last century saw good growth and prosperity, bringing us all necessary goods and some wonderful luxuries. However, it seems like things went too far, we did not learn contentment or restraint and the demon of greed was let out of the bottle.

Two of the most descriptive films of our economic situation were made by moviemaker Oliver Stone - Wall Street 1 and Wall Street 2.

In Wall Street 1 we were introduced to the businessman Gordon Gekko, who was given the opportunity to speak at a shareholders meeting of Teldar Paper. His now famous words seem to still be applicable today. "The point is, ladies and gentlemen, that greed — for lack of a better word — is good. Greed is right. Greed works. Greed clarifies, cuts through, and captures the essence of the evolutionary spirit. Greed, in all of its forms — greed for life, for money, for love, knowledge — has marked the upward surge of mankind. And greed — you mark my words — will not only save Teldar Paper, but that other malfunctioning corporation called the USA."

I think Oliver Stone called his main character Gekko, because this reptile is well-camouflaged. Not easy to recognise, just like greed in today's economy.

Today, we are still trying to clean up the mess of the children of Gordon Gekko. Greed is never good, nor does it serve to work any good purpose. Since we will never be able to attain everything we desire, greed offers us dissatisfaction. Our greediness ultimately destroys us as we harden our hearts, ignoring the needs of others. Ultimately, greed motivates us to pursue poor choices that plunge us into destruction.

"A greedy person tries to get rich quick, but it only leads to poverty[8]."

Our debt-based economy

In 2000, global debt was 87,000 billion US dollars. (In European languages = 'miliard.') At the time of writing, only 19 years later in 2019 it is now at 230'000 billion US dollars, which is three times the world's whole GDP, or it's total economic output, which is approximately 73'500 billion.

To give an idea what a billion really is - If every second a number is pronounced, it takes a full 30 years to count to one billion.

One million in thousands of notes makes a stack of round 10 centimeters of banknotes.

One billion makes a stack of 100 meters. Thousand billion (one trillion) = 100 kilometers

Twenty thousand billion = 20,000 kilometres Banknotes of € 100 notes.

According to the US debt clock[9], the American debt increases by around 50'000 $ every second! This is more than 4 billion $ daily, respectively 1'500'000'000'000 $ annually.

The national debt per capita in the United States (and most other nations has increased rapidly since 1960.

---

8. Proverbs 28:20
9. *http://www.usdebtclock.org*

1960 $1.575; in 2009 - $35.000; and in 2019 - $70.000

These figures make you dizzy, but serve to illustrate the bubble which is being created, and could burst at any time. Why should we worry about the national debt?

First, your social security, pensions and healthcare entitlements are at risk if the national debt continues to grow. Since it will be almost impossible to cut spending and the national debt without touching expensive benefits, your entitlements—especially if you are younger than the Baby Boomers—are very much at risk.

Second, an economic reckoning will come from the explosive growth in national spending and debt. No one really knows how much national debt is too much. Unfortunately, some kind of major economic correction will be the signal that we have gone too far. Other countries will quit buying our debt or will discount it heavily. Stock prices will plunge, and the markets will lose confidence in our reckless fiscal policy. We are creating our own bed of instability when the government spends a lot more than it takes in, and one day the bed will begin to collapse.

Third, spending today and putting it on the tab of the next generation is immoral. Baby Boomers have already made a huge generational transfer of the costs of college, weighing their children down with decades of student debt. Now we are also asking them to pay for our social security and pensions, along with the cost of our collapsing infrastructure and our national defence. But the bill goes forward to our children in a way that is simply wrong. President Herbert Hoover wisely said, "Blessed are the young for they shall inherit the national debt."

Lastly, you should be concerned because the politicians are not.

Since the last crisis, the solution to our problems was found in so-called 'Quantitative Easing,' the creation of huge amounts of money to increase spending and debt-fuelling the economy.

This has led to the creation of free money, governments printing vast amounts of e-money. Money has never been so cheap. From an economic perspective, the printing press is not necessary, as the creation of money primarily shows up electronically on the central bank's balance sheet, on its accounts.

If central banks can potentially create an unlimited amount of money out of thin air, how can we ensure that money remains sufficiently scarce to preserve its value? Does this ability to create money more or less at will not create the temptation to take advantage of this instrument to create additional leeway short term, even at the risk of highly probable long-term damage?

Yes, this temptation certainly does exist, and many in monetary history have succumbed to it. Taking a look back in time, this was often the reason for establishing a central bank: to provide those in power with free access to seemingly unlimited financial resources.

Our economic system is a house of cards. Debt, both household and national is still increasing rapidly. A house based on paper is a crisis waiting to happen.

So, what is the solution? A strong economy in which money plays its part as a medium of exchange, can only be built on what God has created - on real assets - human, natural and relational capital. That is, land, agriculture, real resources such as precious metals and the honest, industrial application of human talent and ingenuity to create value.

Building wealth

Building wealth in Gods economy starts with the God's provision. When Moses was leading the people of Israel into the promised land, he warned them not to forget God who brought them out of slavery, out of the land of 'not enough' into the land of 'more than enough.' He said, "You shall remember the Lord your God, for it is He who gives you power to get wealth, that he may confirm his covenant that he swore to your fathers, as it is this day[10]."

The power to create wealth is a God-given ability, which has a purpose, stated in Moses' command as, 'to confirm His covenant.'

The starting point is the wealth, or capital that God has already given to us. This has five main forms - spiritual capital, physical capital, relational capital, productive capital and financial capital.

Spiritual capital is given to enjoy the pro-activity of God in inspiring, leading, protecting, providing.

Physical capital is given in the form of our strength, health, mental capacity and the earth in which we live, with all its resources.

Relational capital is given in the form of family, friends, colleagues with whom to work together.

Productive capital is given in the form of skills learned, talents and gifts, to produce beneficial goods or services.

Financial capital is given to meet our needs, be generous and share with others and invest for growth.

We must start with the first four types of capital which God provides, develop these first and the money needed to work the system as a form of liquidity will follow. If we, however, focus on money first, the other four will most likely start to become offered on the altar of profit maximisation.

If we concentrate on building on the foundation of the first four capitals God has given, then financial capital will be built also. This can be increased by saving if we do not spend all we earn and learn to be content. Financial capital, and not debt, can be a very safe foundation to build our economy on, both personal and business. Indeed, those families and businesses which survived the crisis of 2008-2015, were those with little or no debt.

---

10. Deuteronomy 8:18

Sustainable prosperity

Right now, in our world economy, we are focussing on creating financial capital of which there is an abundance! Money is cheap and plentiful. We do, however, have a shortage of human, environmental, social, relational and spiritual capitals.

Bruno Roche, top manager at Mars Inc., stated in a speech in the Dutch parliament, that his vision of prosperity in the economy is based on the biblical notions about the Sabbath. "God gave the Ten Commandments to the people of Israel when He led them out of slavery. Thus, we must be freed from our slavery of money." According to Roche, it is a misconception that work is only rewarded with money. "It must be rewarded with rest. It is not for nothing that the words Shemitta (jubilee), Shabbat, Shalom and Shekel have the same origin in Hebrew, and are all forms of remuneration." Shabbat, shekel, shalom and Shemitta (Sabbath year) all come from the same Hebrew root.

Roche, of Judeo-French descent, stated that it has much to say that God in His commandments sets the "Remember the Sabbath Day" before the "Thou shalt not kill" or "Thou shalt not commit adultery". "For man it is good to rest every seventh day, for the land it is good to rest every seventh year. And in order to restore a distorted social distribution of power, God set the year of rejoicing after each 49th year."

The planet provides. Shabbat for land, rest every 7 years

People transform. Shabbat for people, rest every 7 days

Capital ensures liquidity in the system. Shabbat for capital, rest every 7x 7 years

Sustainable prosperity in Gods economy is based on the provision of God, focussing on developing human, social and natural capital and then shared financial capital will follow. Don't follow money, money will follow you. Money is not to accumulate but is meant to facilitate.

Roche propounds the concept of Jubilee, which was given by God because He knew that we need a periodic reset to continue to prosper, and to respect a harmonious remuneration system for the key pillars of economic growth—the planet that provides, the people who transform and add value, and the financial capital to ensure the liquidity in the system.

Jubilee is about setting the captives free, but practically it is about releasing people from overwork and from over-indebtedness. It is about releasing the planet from overuse and overexploitation. It is about releasing wealth from over-accumulation in the hands of a shrinking minority, many of whom are not equipped to contribute entrepreneurially to growing the wealth currently in their hands in ways that go beyond making financial capital with financial capital.

Borrowing wisely

As stated before, the Bible does not forbid borrowing, but warns against many dangers. Debt is 'mammon's banana skin,' a tool mammon uses readily.

In personal borrowing, we can ask ourselves, will it help me to grow and flourish? Do I need something for work or education for which I must borrow? Does it make economic sense? Will the asset which I am purchasing with debt increase in value (such as a home), or help me make increase income?   The economic return must be greater than the cost!

Have I asked for advice? First of all, from my spouse! Husband and wife must be in agreement. "Listen to advice and accept instruction, and in the end you will be wise[11]."

Do I have peace about it? Is it good stewardship of Gods resources?

In business, there are some guidelines to look at. Basically, two principles stand out. They all carry the same biblical principles: Share

---

11. Proverbs 19:20

the risk and do not become bound by personal guarantees. Some questions, you could ask are:

- Can I share the risks? Equity financing, such as venture capital and publicly-traded stock, shares the risk with the business. If the business does not succeed, everyone loses money, even the investors (financiers).

- Can I finance expansion based solely on business collateral? As companies become successful and financially stable, traditional banks are willing to lend money based on the assets of the business alone without any personal guarantees from the shareholders.

- Is supplier financing an option for additional capital? In order for suppliers to increase sales and profitability, they extend credit to certain customers, even longer terms than a standard trade account.

- Can I save out of profits? Savings are probably the best method of financing. Ironically, it is also the least-desired method of financing because it is the most work. Businesses who are financed by the owner's personal savings usually have a much larger chance of success because they have a lot more at stake.

- Can I avoid personal liability? The Bible encourages to avoid personal guarantee. "Be not one of those who give pledges, who put up security for debts. If you have nothing with which to pay, why should your bed be taken from under you[12]?"

---

12. Proverbs 22:26,27

WORK TO SERVE, NOT TO EARN

Working in God's economy is a privilege. Being a Christian does not mean that we are better than anyone else, but we are certainly better off! Not only do we have a new purpose in our work, 'To love God and our neighbour as ourselves,' but also the promise of every resource we will ever need to do all the work God is asking us to do.

Our priority is to "Seek first the (economy of) the Kingdom and His righteousness (the right way of working), then all these things (whatever we need) will be given to you[1]."

When allowing ourselves to 'go with the flow' of the economy of the Kingdom, we need to realise that God is the Provider. One of His many names is 'Jehovah Jireh,' the God who provides our needs; not my employer, or the market, not the customers, nor the banks.

We do not work to earn money, but to love and serve God and our neighbours.

Almighty & Co. Inc.

I have been the subject of a takeover. My life, work and all I am and have been acquired by El Shaddai, the Almighty! "You are not

---

1. Matthew 6:33

your own, for you were bought with a price[2]." This takeover comes complete with all I think I own, money, career, talents, gifts and time. It also comes complete with a takeover of our debt, thanks be to God! This does not only mean my spiritual debt, but also practical debt. I once took over a sizeable business for only one euro. Of course, this came with a sizeable debt, which was the real price of the acquisition. It was then my responsibility as the new owner to reduce the debts of the business to a manageable and healthy level. The Lord will also surely do this for you!

In God's economy, I have been transferred into the Kingdom and the Owner puts me to work in this new enterprise, called "Almighty & Co. Inc." This is a kind of temporary employment agency, which gives me assignments to go and work for this or that business or organisation in the world's economy as a temp, for a specific purpose and for a certain time. I have to give the clients assigned to me my time, effort, talents and gifts in order to receive my income from Almighty & Co. This is an aspect of God's economy which works by giving and receiving, rather than the world's economy which works by buying and selling.

My assignments have been prepared beforehand and my major task is to do my work well, to serve the customers and to uphold the reputation of Almighty in the marketplace. He prepares work that contributes to developing His kingdom in the general economy! "For we are His workmanship, created in Christ Jesus for good works, which God prepared beforehand, that we should walk in them[3]."

In God's economy, we do not work for an income. We work to serve God and to work out His plans. He'll tell us where we're to be working and what to do. We work to serve God! "Whatever you do, work as for the Lord and not for man. You know you will receive the inheritance as a reward[4]."

---

2. 1 Corinthians 6:20
3. Ephesians 2:10
4. Colossians 3:23

If our motivation to work is mainly financial, we serve the wrong master, we serve mammon! Working for income motivates us to choose the job that pays best and not necessarily the job that best suits our unique personality, skills and values. Then we'll miss God's best.

Christian work

The foundation of all economic activity is labour. Labour creates something to be traded or produced and thereby is compensated. Labour is the process through which I reveal my internal reality to the external world. My work reflects and reveals my character, discipline, excellence, commitment to service, and how well I use my God-given gifts.

Working the common kingdom as a Christian may be described as simply human in a general sense. Christians share the life and activities of the common kingdom with all human beings. It is their identification with the redemptive kingdom of God which differentiates them from the rest of humanity. We are not persé better, but we are certainly better off!

We should strive to perform all of our activities in the common kingdom in such a way that is consistent with our Christian identity. We are called not only to act in accordance with God's law at all times, but also to do all things through faith, and to the glory of God. This distinctively separates believers from unbelievers. "Whatever you do, do all to the glory of God[5]."

We should work heartily, as for the Lord and not for men and look to God for our reward[6]. An unbeliever cannot and will not do this. Because of this, we must constantly evaluate all of our work in this light.

The moral requirements for Christians are generally the same as we

---

5. 1 Corinthians 10:31
6. Colossians 3:23

expect of non-Christians; the standards of excellence are the same for believers and unbelievers. We often say that Christian activity should be honest, just, hard-working, environmentally responsible, and respectful to authority. This is certainly true, but it is also true for unbelievers. Of course, these qualities are only to be expected because humanity in general has been created in the likeness of God and are expressions of the characteristics of God in all people. All human beings continue to bear the image of God, albeit with a tendency to sin, and morally obligated to God. All people continue to know the basic moral law of God because it is written on their hearts[7].

Similarly, the standards of excellence for our work are generally the same for unbelievers as for believers. What constitutes excellence for a Christian engineer? Are these different from a non-Christian engineer? I would rather be treated by an excellent non-Christian competent dentist than by a Christian dentist who does not understand his work! Activities such as building houses or maintaining roads are general human activities, not uniquely Christian ones. These are activities of the common kingdom.

Scripture tells us little or nothing about details of working activities or how these should be carried out. Making concrete decisions in economics and business requires wisdom and judgement in the light of the circumstances. It is likely that no two Christians would take the same decision about how to market their products, whether to hire or fire certain people, how to reduce their tax bill, or to move their premises to a different location. Is there such thing as a Christian business? Or are there just businesses which are run by Christians?

Vocation

For us as Christians our productive work is a vocation. This indicates that our work is a calling. God is the one who calls us to productive work, however mundane to serve Him and my neighbour. Productive labour is ordained by God and is inherently dignified. Work, whether

---

7. Romans 1:18 to 32, 2:14 – 15.

sweeping streets, washing dishes, or leading the government, has the blessing of God when it is lawful and carried out conscientiously.

God called Adam and his descendants to work. After Adam disobeyed, his work was to fall under a curse and be subject to pain and frustration. After the flood, God reaffirmed in the covenant given to Noah, that all human beings bear his image, albeit in a fallen and corrupted way, and therefore would continue to pursue various vocational tasks. Human work therefore belongs to the common kingdom. Occupations such as farming, metalworking, music, belong not only to believers but to all in common. Jabal, Jubal and Tubal-Cain excelled in all of these[8].

As they pursue their daily vocations, out of faith in Christ and to the glory of God, God calls most of us to work in businesses and organisations that are institutions of the common kingdom.

It is important to recognise, that while Christians themselves are redeemed as citizens of the kingdom of God, their daily vocations are not. While work of all sorts is intrinsically valuable, meaningful, and God honouring, we are not building the new heaven and a new earth; and we labour in this present world which is transient and fleeting. However, we can influence work in the common kingdom by following the leadership and empowering of the Holy Spirit to bring salt, light, leaven to the world's economy.

In a profound way Jean Valjean, the hero from Victor Hugo's "Les Miserables" embodies "vocation, meaning and ethics." The words become flesh in his life. After his encounter with the bishop's amazing grace, he begins to find a new way to understand his life, and the life of the world around him. Over the next years his whole community is transformed by his visionary leadership in building a business that offers opportunity and employment, and whose product serves the marketplace. Valjean becomes a remarkably kind man with eyes to see the needs of those in his community, but that is as a businessman with a strong sense of vocation grounded in an understanding of the

---

8. Genesis 4:20-22

meaning of life manifest in an ethic that has consequence for him and his world.

Avodah

This is a key Hebrew word which gives us understanding about work in the Kingdom economy. *Avodah* is used in the beginning of Genesis where it is the Hebrew word for "work." We read, "There was no man to work the ground," and, "The Lord God took the man and put him in the Garden of Eden to work it[9]." *Avodah* is used again in Genesis 4:2 when God says, "Cain worked the soil."

Avodah is God's word for "work."

In fact, in the Hebrew Bible, avodah has three dimensions. The Hebrew word *avodah* jointly means work, worship, and service.

Firstly, just hard work, as the children of Israel had to struggle hard for the construction of Pharaoh's cities under appalling conditions. Secondly, to serve and worship God as the servants in the Temple led the worship with their commitment. Thirdly, *avodah* means serving others with your gifts and talents. These three dimensions should live seamlessly together. We work to serve God and our neighbour, and because we love God and want to bring honour to Him.

The Ancient Hebrews had a deep understanding of how faith and work came together in their lives. It shouldn't be surprising, then, that they used the same word for work, for serving others and for worshipping God. These three are inextricably linked.

Working without serving people is lost work. This is frustrating, hard and makes you ask the question, 'what am I doing this for?'

Working without meaning is destructive - you have to make people feel like they're working on something big. The story is told about a Bishop who was passing by the new building site and stopped to look

---

9. Genesis 2:5, 15

at what several stone cutters were doing. He asked the first, "What are you doing?" "Cutting stone," was the reply. The Bishop asked the second one the same question. "I am placing the stones together to build a wall." The Bishop asked the third one. "What are you doing?" "I am building a cathedral," said the stone mason. He was quickly promoted!

For several years, I managed a business conducting special contracts for the European Space Agency. I know that our contracts, organising safety on the shuttle and space station formed just a small part of the overall missions. We told our staff, "You are helping to sustain life in space, to improve life on earth." Their work had a much bigger impact than merely their own small contribution. It is important to give all our co-workers a larger vision.

In the well-loved story of the 'Little Prince,' the writer, Antoine St. Expert, who lost his life as a pilot in WW2, illustrated this point. "If you want to build a ship, do not call together men in order to get wood, prepare tools, allocate jobs and organize work; but teach them a longing for the fascinating, endless world."

Bezalel, the prototype of a Christian worker!

The first person to receive the Holy Spirit in the Bible was Bezalel. He was not a prophet, not a Bible teacher, not a leader, but a worker with his hands. His name means, 'in the shadow of God'. He probably was put to hard labour in the building programmes of the Pharaoh. After Moses had led the people of Israel out of slavery, Bezalel was called by name for a very special task - to build the tabernacle, the very first 'dwelling' of God on earth.

It is not difficult to think that God saw his faith, loyalty, attitude and skill in Egypt, and saw in him the ideal person to build the tabernacle. A sanctuary for worship, the tabernacle was to be the place of God's presence in the midst of Israel. People were invited to see God there, to experience God's holiness and glory. The tabernacle, built with the finest materials, was to reflect the beauty of God's character.

"Behold, I have called Bezalel, son of Uri, son of Hur, out of the tribe of Judah, by his name. I have filled him with the Spirit of God, with wisdom, insight, knowledge and all kinds of craftsmanship, to devise designs and to carry them out in gold, silver and copper; and to work and use precious stones, and to work in wood, that is to say, to do all kinds of work[10].

God, our employer, endorses us with the Spirit of God for the work he gives us to do. This endorsement includes wisdom, insight, knowledge and craftsmanship! He would work with God's Spirit in the economy of God's kingdom. Leonardo da Vinci said, "Where the Spirit does not work by hand, there is no art."

From start to finish, building the tabernacle was a God given process, and our work can be the same. Every detail of the structure reflects the divine will and nothing rests on *ad hoc* decisions of human builders. There is no tension whatever between form and content, or symbol and reality throughout the chapters describing the making of the tabernacle. The tabernacle with its contents was the subject of much divine thought and care. I believe the Lord gives our work this same care and attention.

Specifically, the Lord gives Bezalel five dimensions of work. Wisdom, insight, knowledge, creativity and execution.

Wisdom, which is the Bible word '*hokmah*,' reflects knowing how and knowing when - being smart. It reflects an insight into God's heart and creativity, to be able to distinguish and discern what is right, to understand problems and how to solve them.

The Spirit gave Bezalel knowledge of materials and ways to work them, technology. He was endowed with creativity, performing in small ways what God does in His creation, to create beauty and solve problems. Lastly, the Spirit enabled Bezalel to execute the plans, the

---

10. Exodus 31:2-5

ability to get things done, to manage co-workers, and finish the work.

Bezalel's name means, 'in the shadow of God.' You and I are now working in the shadow of God, just like Bezalel. Our motivation is to serve people with the mind of Christ. Our work is a preparation for 'eternal work' in the new heaven and on the new earth. Jesus is our chief... He gives us assignments and the necessary resources to finish the work. We don't learn in church how to be a good carpenter... but we should learn that being a good carpenter is a requirement in following Jesus! Dorothy Sayers said, "The church's approach to an intelligent carpenter is usually confined to moral instruction and church attendance. What the church should be telling him is this: the very first demand that his religion has on him is that he should make good tables!"

For the Hebrews, working is ultimately religion in action. We see in Bezalel the transformation of work, from slavery in Egypt to empowerment and freedom to build for God. The Spirit will help you to become free to use your gifts and talents to the glory of God in a way which brings meaning to your life and serves your neighbours.

The power of compassion

In the end nothing less than love, love in the sense of caring with heart and soul, of being involved in the other person, is behind compassion - *caritas*.

And that whole concept is of course not popular today. Left-wing people are happy that we are finally freed from charity because the state is making it better. Right-wing conservatives want to bring much of the care back to the private sphere, to the charities. But there's one thing left and right agree on: *caritas* is a concept from and for the private sphere. It has no place in the big world of society, politics and economics. There it is about results, about money, about power.

In old cities you will find beautiful historic buildings and they are worth a visit. But if you want to renovate something or if there is a risk that things will collapse, then it becomes very difficult when you no longer have the building plans. What is a load-bearing wall and what can you get rid of? Or, another example, a Stradivarius is and remains a beautiful violin. We know quite a lot about the maker's technique, but the real secret of his violins - we don't remember. We need to rediscover the foundational pillar of love, the secret of the violin, which is largely absent from the common economy, but which should be prominent in Gods economy!

Agapé (love) is the pillar of our society, it is the secret of the melodious Stradivarius, and public love is essential for social renewal.

Love is of course already an important word in the Old Testament and in the New it becomes the centre of everything: *Agapé*. You won't believe it, but that whole word didn't exist in the Greek world. The translators of the Septuagint had to invent it to be able to say something in Greek like '*ahav*' - to love God because He loves us and your neighbour as yourself. There was not a word for that: you had *eros* for a sexual love, and *philia* for a connection with your peers. Aristotle considered friendship between God and man impossible, because *philia* can only occur between equals. But there was no word for that love that bridges the biggest gap between God and man. There are still no words for that, you might say, but the translators forged the word *agapé* for it. And for all New Testament writers, this new concept with old roots became the way to indicate God's love in Christ and the love of Christians across borders.

Adam Smith, father of market thinking, had beautiful ideals related to seeking the good of your neighbour, but failed to verify that "the market" always works so lovingly. And in a broader sense, it is quite risky to build structures that should shape love. Then, with a word from T.S. Eliot, you're working on "dreaming of systems so perfect that no one will need to be good".

Many Christian 'points of view' have unfortunately been lost and long forgotten, but love remains. Love as a building plan in this case.

Imagine the end of a day's sales conference at a large insurance company. The invited keynote speaker gets up and delivers this bombshell: "Everything you've heard so far is not true." Tony Campolo, professor emeritus of sociology at Eastern University in Pennsylvania, opened his speech with this statement after some power speakers had instructed the audience on how to animate customers; to 'set up' clients, 'push the right emotional buttons,' and 'close the deal.' Tony's task was to "psych up" the audience for a last big motivational push. You can imagine the shock when he said, "Everything you've heard so far is not true!"

"People are not things to be manipulated with the right techniques," he said, "not economic objects; they are entitled to love." The audience was enthralled as he made a case to make "love" a verb demonstrated daily in the office and the factory.

The most powerful force in business isn't greed, fear, or even the raw energy of unbridled competition. The most powerful force in business is love - the selfless promotion of the growth of the other. This is truly counter-cultural and swimming against the flow.

Tony Campolo described love at work in a very practical paraphrase of 1 Corinthians 13:

"Although I have the communication skills of men and angels and have not love, I sound just like a clanging cymbal. If I can predict business trends and have a total grasp of the latest production techniques and have the kind of positive thinking that people say is the secret of success but have no love, it really does no lasting good. And although I make all the sacrifices so that there can be better wages for my workers, and make sure they have all the fringe benefits possible and do not show them love, it will still leave them grumbling and discontented. Love teaches me to put up with a lot of things that would ordinarily make me angry, and it makes me into a listening, sensitive person. It keeps me from acting like a big shot and going on ego trips. Love keeps me from being rude to even the lowliest person in the company. It keeps me from demanding that things always be done my way; it keeps me from blowing up at the least little thing. And it prevents me from keeping files on all the mistakes made by people working for me. Love gets no satisfaction out of the failures of others—even when their failures guarantee that I will get a promotion."

GIVING & RECEIVING VS BUYING & SELLING

"A man may give freely, and still his wealth will be increased; and another may keep back more than is right, but only comes to be in need[1]."

God's economy works by giving and receiving; the economy of the common kingdom by buying and selling! The Bible teaches us that the world economy of buying and selling is going to get such a strong grip that there will be a situation in which we will not get a share in economic traffic, unless we participate in a perverse trading system (with Babylon as a symbol) that will eventually fall. We are already living at the beginning of this process!

The Bible says that there will come a time when it will be made impossible to buy and sell unless we carry 'the brand of the Beast'; and in that time the souls of people will be sold[2]!

The mechanism of buying and selling, if not curbed by God's economy, can lead to manipulation and ultimately to enslavery of people. Think only of modern slavery in the factories of Bangladesh and the sale of young girls into prostitution, and we realise these times are not far off!

This does not mean that the system of buying and selling in the general kingdom is wrong. It has been controlled by the fact that it

---

1. Proverbs 11:24
2. Revelation 13:17 & 18:13

is a contractual system that is subject to certain accepted standards and legal rules. We, as citizens and strangers, can engage in buying and selling based on these accepted standards and laws in such a contractual system with respect for the rules and for the interests of the other.

The economy of the kingdom of God works with a covenant system, which gives an extra dimension to the contractual system. For example, learning to give, looking for the best interests for the other person, doing good, considering the other person more excellent than yourself, walking the extra mile are actions which introduce people into the economy of God's kingdom.

Love turns out to be an important economic value. Love is risky. Love gives others freedom and responsibility and is willing to bear the pain that can result from the risks. Love endures everything[3]. It's all about granting forgiveness when things go wrong. Taking risks by trusting people is an essential prerequisite for entrepreneurship and a creative economy, of great importance in a rapidly changing, dynamic society. Love and therefore entrepreneurship is "gift exchange".

Buying and selling in the economy of the general kingdom is held under control by the righteousness of acceptable norms and laws, but also made pleasant and beneficial by giving and receiving, the covenant system of God's economy. Giving and receiving lead to healthy relationships.

Jesus was once subjected to the economy of buying and selling in the general kingdom. In this case, this kingdom was led by a Roman governor, Pilate, and executed by religious leaders, the Pharisees, who the Bible tells us were lovers of money.

Jesus was sold once by Judas for 30 pieces of silver and he was bought by the Pharisees. This was the price of a slave in the economy of the general kingdom. This then led to his death. At the cross several powers were present; political power in the form of Pilate, religious

---

3. 1 Corinthians 13:7

power in the form of the Pharisees, military power in the form of the soldiers and also financial power - mammon was there in an apparent victory.

The victory, however, was won by Jesus. "He disarmed the rulers and authorities and put them to open shame, by triumphing over them in him[4]." Mammon was conquered!

Jesus was subjected to the economy of the general kingdom, to the contract of purchase and sale, so that through his death and resurrection he might bring us into the economy of the kingdom of God, into an economy of giving and receiving, an economy of grace!

Prof. Jacques Ellul, says in his book 'Money and Power,' "The selling of Jesus, first foreshadowed by the story of Joseph sold by his brothers, then by Amos (2:6), shows the constancy of the selling relationship and carries it's meaning to the absolute. This sale defines all selling. They sold the Righteous. This act, which is our act, is reflected in each selling relationship. Now all money affairs are characterised by the fact that Jesus became the object of a money relationship. And because the Son of God was thus turned into merchandise, all subordination of humankind to money is intolerable."

One economist said, "We don't need to be educated about economics, but rather we need salvation from it!" Through the contractual system of buying and selling, Mammon ultimately wants to enslave us; the Holy Spirit wants to set us free!

Saved from the buying and selling mechanism

This means that I do not have to be subject to the market economy of buying and selling any more.

God's economy works by giving and receiving. The Bible teaches us that the economy of buying and selling will get such a strong grip

---

4. Colossians 2:15

on the world economy, that we will not be able to participate in economic life unless we conform to the standards of our perverse trading system, with Babylon as a symbol, which will eventually fall. We are living at the beginning of this process.

We see Jesus operating in a way which was not in line with what we would expect when he was so mad at the moneychangers. Uncharacteristically, Jesus was extremely angry at this business going on. The place where this happened is significant. It took place in the Court of the Gentiles, which was the area in the Temple to which non-Jews could come to meet God and receive grace. Where grace should be freely given, mammon reigned. This business showed the corrupt nature of the buying and selling process. Although you would think that the moneychangers were giving a good service for pilgrims who had come from afar to change money to buy sacrifices, the service was, in fact, servitude to mammon. Products of poor quality were being sold in the form of blemished and therefore unacceptable animals for sacrifice. Inflated prices and unfair exchange rates lined the pockets of the controlling Pharisees, whom Jesus described as "lovers of money[5]."

Mammon is called the unrighteous mammon. Therefore, every transaction will be subject to unrighteousness, to have the characteristic of going wrong somewhere and at some time. This temptation brings selfishness, corruption, lying, stress and anxiety.

The buying and selling relationship has another characteristic, it profanes that which is sacred. That is, it violates, desecrates or debases the Kingdom activities of giving and receiving.

The prophecy of Ezekiel about Tyre, probably the world's first multinational trading empire, strongly and clearly reveals that commerce ends up by 'profaning what is sacred.' After having described at length Tyre's imports and exports, all its trade which leads to power (chapters 26-27), Ezekiel concludes: "By the multitude of your iniquities, in the unrighteousness of your trade

---

5. Luke 16:14

you profaned your sanctuaries[6]"

Remember you do not work for a living, but for a giving ...

The concept of giving and receiving in the economy of the Kingdom has liberated me from the pressures of selling. I have always worked in commercial ventures and, surprisingly, found the sales process always very stressful. So, how does this work? I am called to give to my customers the best of my talents, experience, skills, gifts and serve them to meet their needs and to help them achieve their goals. In return, I will receive out of God's provision, what I need for the continuation of the business. God instructs companies or people to pay me ... if they don't ... they will have to deal with God!

Giving & receiving leads to healthy and strong relationships.

Using mammon

We must use what mammon offers. We must neither neglect nor refuse it. When we enter mammon's territory, when we receive money, his channel of power, when we are involved in buying and selling, are we going to obey the law of money, are we going to continue the circle of mutual sales, in other words, are we then going to adopt allegiance to mammon?

The very thing Jesus asks here is that we maintain our allegiance to God. This faithfulness to God is not reserved for spiritual things; it must be engraved on the things of the world.

Allegiance to God must penetrate the world of money. When we enter this world, we must be attached to Jesus Christ in order not to adopt its law, just as Christ, when he entered our world, did not adopt the law of sin even though it is inscribed in human flesh.

 Here then we have two worlds, one of selling and one of giving, totally opposed to each other and therefore strangers and without

---

6. Ezekiel 28:18

communication with each other. Jesus asks us to penetrate the world of selling in order to penetrate it with grace by our faithfulness to God, the only Master. Grace must use the very instruments that are customary in the world of selling. Grace must invade the power of money, for when mammon is destroyed by grace, it is no longer a formidable power.

Jesus commanded us to 'make friends with the unrighteous mammon[7],' to use money to help people to be set free and to achieve their God-given potential. Sometimes, this may mean using our money, according to the world's standards 'uneconomically.' Forgiving a debt, giving extra discount, acts of generosity are not good business, if maximization of your income is the main focus!

Bringing grace into business

A wonderful picture of grace is Victor Hugo's story, 'Les Misérables.' In this, Valjean, an ex-convict on parole, embittered by the discrimination he received everywhere he went because of his criminal status, had just been taken in for the night by a Bishop after being kicked out of everywhere else he had found to stay. In response to the mercy shown to him, however, Valjean robbed the Bishop's house and in the night, ran away with some silverware. He was soon caught by the police, to whom he then lied that the Bishop had made a present of the silver. Not believing him, the police brought him back to the Bishop's house to test the story, and secure Valjean's indictment. However, instead of taking his silver back and condemning Valjean, the Bishop tells the officers that he had indeed given the silver to Valjean, and not only that, he offered some additional candlesticks that Valjean had 'forgotten' in his haste to leave! In his zeal to redeem Valjean, not just in person but also in spirit, the Bishop had indeed turned the other cheek after being slapped in the face, and 'given his cloak when asked for his shirt.[7]' Valjean, unable to comprehend this radical act of grace

---

7. Luke 16:9

shown to him, renounces his old life and follows the Bishop's command to 'use this precious silver to become an honest man.'

The Bishop drew near to Valjean, and said, "Jean Valjean, my brother, you no longer belong to evil, but to good. It is your soul that I buy from you; I withdraw it from black thoughts and the spirit of perdition, and I give it to God." Valjean was redeemed by grace and entered into a new reality. That is the purpose of using money uneconomically; to introduce people into God's world of grace. Is it possible to 'buy back' someone's soul through acts of selfless kindness? That is exactly what Jesus did for you and me.

Mammon would have us focus on maximising our financial resources instead of giving them away. When the goal of any activity is solely financial, we are serving the wrong Lord. The goal must first be service and then the fulfilment of financial needs will follow. Our focus must be fixed on the question, "How do I become a blessing to others, rather than how do I receive a blessing."

This Old Testament story of Ruth and Boaz speaks loudly to common grace in the workplace. It would have been unlikely for these two characters to meet. Still, sovereign God had plans for them to play an important role in moving redemptive history forward. Ruth was at Moabite and Boaz was an Israelite. These two peoples traditionally had little to do with one another.

Boaz goes out of his way to provide and protect this Moabite woman of whom he knew little. He had only heard of her loyal commitment to her mother in law, Naomi. At this time, I doubted Boaz had any idea how his many tangible acts of unselfish kindness and grace offered to Ruth in the workplace would be used by God. Through Ruth and Boaz, the line leading to King David would be established, and through the line of David, Jesus the Messiah would come.

It was a custom in the Old Testament economy that owners of land fostered the common good by leaving a portion of their crops in the fields for the poor to harvest as a way for them to work and provide for their needs. Boaz owned fields and allowed Ruth to glean, taking some of the crops to sustain her family.

In a sales seminar, I remember being reminded that we could get more out of a deal if we had pushed just that little bit further! The principle of 'leaving some on the table' means to refrain from taking the utmost advantage of something; to not squeeze every last drop from a deal; but to 'leave money on the table', to be willing to negotiate a deal that is less financially beneficial than is expected or possible.

The Law of Reciprocity

Reciprocity is a type of relationship in which individuals relate to one another based on an interest in each other. The purpose of this type of relationship is to obtain mutual benefits through their giving and receiving.

A basic tenet in the psychology of relationships is called the Principle of Reciprocity. This principle basically defines the human need and tendency to want to give something back when something is received. This need is strongest when the gift is given without expectation of return. But even at the lowly (but important) level of simple social graces, a 'thank you' (in response to an act of kindness or compliment) is still followed by another reciprocal gesture of accommodation 'you're welcome.'

Very early in my sales career a wise mentor told me that being successful in business is akin to putting effort into the front end of a very long, dark pipe and reaping rewards from the other end. The rewards we reap are in direct proportion to the effort we expend. This is the Law of Reciprocity. And it's called by many names. In one of his essays, Brian Tracy explained this principle:

"Perhaps the most powerful principle of all in personal influence is contained in what is called the Law of Reciprocity. It is also called the Law of Sowing and Reaping, and the Law of Action and Reaction." Napoleon Hill called it the Law of Overcompensation. Probably the best summary of the Law of Reciprocity is the Golden Rule, which says, "Do unto others as you would have them do unto you, to love others as you love yourself[8]." The most common explanation of this in our economy today is 'Those who have the gold, make the rules!'

Ralph Waldo Emerson observed, "It is one of the most beautiful compensations in life that no man can sincerely try to help another without helping himself." An eastern proverb says, "The hand that washes another will become clean itself."

Finally, one of our most prolific late 20th century poets, Paul McCartney phrased it simply, "And, in the end, the love you take is equal to the love you make."

This principle is immutable. Like the Law of Gravity, whether you choose to "believe" it, matters not. The force of gravity works just as effectively on those who recognise it as on those who are ignorant to its effects. And so it is with The Law of Reciprocity.

The basis for developing remarkable relationships is really nothing more than remembering your customers and clients are - at the heart of it - people. This means they have hopes, disappointments, joys, tragedies, worries and victories…just like you.

Your customers are people – not businesses, shops, factories or schools. They need to be able to trust you. Trust is one of the most important aspects of doing business. It has everything to do with reputation and a good name. It takes long to build up trust, but it can be easily destroyed. Building rapport is a sympathetic connection to win their hearts. Many a deal has been granted solely on the basis that a buyer likes the salesman and wants to do business with him. With trust comes favour – the goodwill and approval without which we won't succeed in business! The principle of reciprocity means to give and take for each other's benefit; give and it will be given to you. It means granting favour first of all to the customer to build up a strong personal relationship. This brings grace into human relationships!

---

8. Luke 6:31

The Principle of Reciprocity describes a human need for give and take in a relationship. In order for the "gift" to have the most meaning, it needs to be offered in a way that is genuine, without the expectation of return. But in business, there is an expectation of return; therefore, the Principle of Reciprocity should be built on trust by offering incentives to customers, but also by offering customer service and complaint resolution policies that inspire that trust.

Become a skilful listener. Simply by taking your eyes off of yourself and paying attention to other people, you'll be amazed at the things you'll discover about others.

Economics of mutuality

I was privileged to be with Bruno Roche, Chief Economist at Mars Inc. at a meeting of the European Economic Summit, which I helped to create. He proposed an 'economics of mutuality.' This is based on the value of the individual.

Starting with the value of the individual, the first task is to develop and invest in Human Capital. Then in the way each individual relates to and interacts with others to develop Social Capital with shared identity and values. And then this should be developed within the framework of our Natural Capital, investing in environmental capital. Lastly, this all leads to developing financial capital.

Bruno Roche stated that if we start with developing Financial Capital as the primary goal, then this will always transpire to the cost of human capital, social capital and environmental capital. Financial Capital is the fruit of investing in human, social and natural capital and is only needed for liquidity in the system, to facilitate exchange.

Roche, "Marxism only wanted to pay the people at the expense of the others; Greens only want to pay the land at the expense of the others: and modern capitalism only wants to pay the capital at the expense of the others!"

This is merely a re-iteration of the creation order! Firstly, God created the earth and gave it to man to provide and enjoy! That is natural, environmental capital. Then, God created man to enjoy the creation and develop this natural capital. He wanted people to grow and develop their gifs and talents - human capital. Then God observed that it was 'not good that man should be alone,' and created woman. Social capital was born! Financial capital only came as a means of facilitating the exchange of goods and services allowing the economy to grow. The purpose of money is not to accumulate but to facilitate!

Roche, "Focus on developing human, social and natural capital and the shared financial capital will follow. Don't follow money, money will follow you."

Almost all economic systems throughout the ages have been based on three things: the land that provides the resources and raw materials from which goods can be made, the people who transform these resources into goods and services that can be sold and the financial capital (money) that provides liquidity to the system. These are the three pillars of prosperity in any economic and business situation.

Roche, "Marxism remunerated people first, which eventually took place at the expense of financial capital and the health of the planet. Financial capitalism, following the Friedman school, by contrast, rewards the holders of financial capital at the expense of people (the many)—unless they are shareholders (the few)—and at the expense of the planet. And some today, propose to remunerate the planet at the expense of financial capital and of people."

The Economics of Mutuality asks the question: How do we do business with a new business model approach that delivers superior business performance by mobilising and managing the different forms of capital beyond just money?

Mutually sharing the benefits from business involves all interested parties. The economics of mutuality maintains that growth is not linked to how much one earns, but how much is shared.

Mutuality - giving and receiving - was emphasised by Martin Luther

King. "In a real sense all life is interrelated. All men are caught in an inescapable network of mutuality, tied in a single garment of destiny. Whatever affects one directly, affects all indirectly. I can never be what I ought to be until you are what you ought to be, and you can never be what you ought to be until I am what I ought to be... This is the interrelated structure of reality."

Let us use our financial capital to set people free, enabling them to enjoy Human, Social and Natural Capital in all they do! That is economics of mutuality ... mutual remuneration ... so that each individual involved in the economic process experiences Shalom ...peace, contentment, completeness, wholeness, well-being and harmony!

Receiving in Gods economy

"So I gave you a land on which you did not toil and cities you did not build; and you live in them and eat from vineyards and olive groves that you did not plant[9] "

Theologian Ched Myers talks about 'Sabbath economics' as the basic struggle of mammon vs. manna. Mammon is translated as 'money' or 'wealth' in many Bible translations and is portrayed a few verses later as the "love of money[10]." Mammon is then illustrated by a tale Jesus tells[11], in which a rich man feasts sumptuously and stores up luxury goods even as a poor beggar lies right outside his door. The economy of mammon is one of excess accumulation for some and poverty and deprivation for others.

"Manna," on the other hand, refers to the story from Exodus 16 in which God rains down "bread from heaven[12]." The Hebrew people were instructed to gather neither too much nor too little of the manna, but rather enough to meet their needs. And they were not to

---

9. Joshua 24:13
10. Luke 16:14
11. Luke 16:19-31
12. Exodus 16:4

gather manna on the Sabbath day itself, making this manna story one of the first illustrations in all scripture of the meaning of Sabbath. In contrast to mammon economics of excess and deprivation, this model of manna or "Sabbath" economics stresses God's abundance and provision. That abundance carries with it the accompanying instruction not to gather too much lest others go without.

God provided Manna (which literally means, "What is this?") for food, and instructed the Israelites to gather enough food on the 6th day to provide for the 7th (Sabbath) - but not to gather extra on the other days of the week. If they gathered more than they needed, the food would spoil and smell vile.

Abraham Heschel stated, "There are few ideas in the world of thought which contain so much spiritual power as the idea of Sabbath. No matter what the restrictions, Sabbath is a time when the goal is: not to have but to be; not to own but to give; not to control but to share and not to subdue but to serve."

God's provision in the economy of the Kingdom, is not based on what we earn or deserve but solely on His grace, unmerited favour. This is described beautifully here. "Come, everyone who thirsts, come to the waters; and he who has no money, come, buy and eat! Come, buy wine and milk without money and without price. Why do you spend your money for that which is not bread, and your labour for that which does not satisfy? Listen diligently to me, and eat what is good, and delight yourselves in rich food[13].."

---

13. Isaiah 55:1,2

CONTENTMENT & ENOUGH VS PROGRESS & MORE

The Rolling Stones were famous for their complaint, "I can't get no satisfaction," no matter how hard they tried! Satisfaction is a wonderful thing!

I recently read a short article from a young professional lady, Renate Rijsenberg. She says, "In recent weeks I discussed the issue of finances with people around me. During a dinner with family, at work, and in a relaxed evening with friends, I asked a few questions, kept my ears open and noticed what people had to say."

"First of all, I was amazed at the taboo hanging around the topic of money. It is always a bit vague. Telling your salary is 'not-done', the state of your bank account is very private. We only tell others when we have made a bargain buy or bought a mega-expensive product." "… And truth be known, I feel the same. The more I earn, the more I need to make ends meet. You constantly strive to earn more, to give your family more, taking a vacation at least twice a year, live in a beautiful house with a large garden, ride a nice car, have enough savings in the bank and, if possible share with everyone."

"Money is playing such a huge role in our society, that it seems like you don't count any more if you don't have 'enough' money. And even if you do have all the things I just mentioned, then the question remains if all this satisfies you."

The basis of contentment and satisfaction is having enough. Every Christian should answer this question of "how much is enough?" for themselves. This is a very easy question to ask but difficult to answer, but the answer, when found, will lead to the ability to realise what the most important things in our lives are.

The Greek philosopher Epicurus stated, "nothing is enough, for the man to whom enough is too little." Contrast that with the well-known answer to our question from J.D. Rockefeller, which although stated over a hundred years ago, seems to have characterised our capitalist system recently. When asked 'how much is enough' he stated, 'just a little bit more!'

From time to time a friend goes to a rural monastery for a silent retreat. Meals are provided by the monks. The many acres of wooded land are laced with walking trails. There are several small sanctuaries with just a chair or two. Each room has a bed, a desk, a chair, a lamp, and no more. The atmosphere is one of silence and peace. On one retreat he asked himself, "If I knew that everyone in the world would have enough, if I had only this much, would this be enough for me?

I've noticed a few consistent qualities in the lives of people who have come to know how much is enough for them.

1. They have a sense of purpose larger than their own needs, wants and desires. Desires are infinite. Fill one desire and another emerges. A sense of purpose, though, sorts real needs from whims and preferences and directs your attention to only those things that will really serve your mission – whether the "mission" is raising children, a garden, money or consciousness.

2. They can account for their money. They know where it comes from and where it goes. There's a sense of clarity that comes from such precision and truthfulness. If you don't know how much you have, you can never have enough. Without a purposefully and prayerfully designed budget, there will not be money left over for generosity or long-term goals.

3. They have an internal yardstick for fulfilment. Their sense

of 'enoughness' isn't based on what others have or don't have (keeping up with the Joneses, or down with the Ethiopians). It's based on a capacity to look inside and see if something is really adding to their happiness, or is it just more stuff to store, insure, fix, forget about and ultimately sell in a garage sale.

4. Like my friend at the dinner table in the monastery, they have a sense of responsibility for the world, a sense of how their lives and choices fit into the larger social and spiritual scheme of things.

The Law of Diminishing Returns

The law of Diminishing Return is, "The tendency for a continuing application of effort or skill toward a particular project or goal to decline in effectiveness, after a certain level of result has been achieved."

The law means that the more people earn, the less they will be inclined to work extra, since the financial 'good' of additional earnings comes increasingly at the cost of other 'goods', such as leisure and family time. A very high proportion of women in The Netherlands work part-time because of childcare needs. Working more would yield less 'good' for them. Looking at it from a different angle, having reached a certain level of national income, we might conceivably take the opportunity to begin prioritising other things. Our stagnant economy has serious problems, not least the size of its debts.

The Law of Diminishing Returns could be illustrated by what I call the Fulfilment Curve. If we plot fulfilment against money spent in a Gauss curve, we see first a sharp rise in fulfilment with the ability to spend to meet basic needs. The Bible talks about *food & clothing*[1],' 'your wages[2],'and *'with what you have*[3].'

---

1. 1 Timothy 6:8
2. Luke 3:14
3. Hebrews13:5

The curve continues to rise as we spend on basic comforts. Paul tells Timothy that God is a generous God *"… who gives us all things richly to enjoy*[4].*"*

However, as we transition into spending more on luxuries, the return on our extra spending tails off … as we move into consumerism, experiencing the lack of fulfilment we have just discussed.

The key is to determine the point at which more spending does not bring more satisfaction. When is it enough? At that point, more spending will not bring more happiness., so then we should stop spending any more. Satisfaction can then be attained by investing in people and in Gods Kingdom, by being generous.

The antidote to consumerism and the door to living 'the good life' is answering the question, "How Much Is Enough"? If we determine the threshold of enough, income over and above that can be utilised to build assets with which to invest in doing good – first of all to our family and friends and then to the world at large.

Answering the question, will put a stop to excessive spending and allow us to build up assets with which we can do good. A prayer from Agur in Proverbs is very applicable. *".. give me neither poverty nor riches; feed me with the food that is needful for me, lest I be full and deny you and say, "Who is the Lord?" or lest I be poor and steal and profane the name of my God*[5].*"*

The way out of this downward spiral of consumerism, materialism and discontent is to grow in generosity, because Jesus explained very simply …" you are happier and more blessed when you give than when you receive[6]."

---

4. 1 Timothy 6:17
5. Proverbs 30:8,9
6. Acts 20:32

Prosperity with a purpose

Our culture trains us to think that wealth typically refers only to financial assets and worldly possessions.

A moment's reflection shows us that a well-lived life (we could call it true wealth) is about much more than finances.

For example, if you become a millionaire but lose all your friends and family, are you wealthy? Is that a good trade-off? Is that a well-lived life? Is it worth losing friends to get more money? If you make more money than everyone else in the world but live in a house by yourself all day with an incurable illness that gives you chronic pain, are you wealthy? Is that a good life? How much money is chronic pain worth? Would you rather have a rich teacher or a wise teacher?

I think most of us would agree that a life isn't good if it's filled with financial prosperity but no other kind of flourishing.

Our problem, then, is that our measurement of wealth is too small. It's not that we shouldn't look for a return on our investments; it's that we need to expand our definition of what kind of return we're looking for. We need a new way of evaluating and measuring what actually happens when we make these kinds of investments. We need to think *much wider* about prosperity and wealth.

In 3 John 2, where John prays that the recipient of the letter would prosper in 'all respects' and that he would be in good health, 'just as your soul prospers.' The writer is giving us a holistic view of prosperity that is a helpful corrective against the short-sighted focus of the so-called prosperity gospel. John is saying that *every area of your life should prosper*, not just one or two. He describes prosperity in terms of multiple kinds of capital and currency,

This way of looking at prosperity helps keep everything in proper orientation and guards us against the excesses of a narrow focus on only one area of capital apart to the detriment of the others. The problem with prosperity theology is that it doesn't aim high enough. It's narrowly focused on measuring financial prosperity when it ought to be thinking about spiritual, relational, physical, and productive prosperity, too. It follows the way of the world in valuing financial capital above all else, instead of recognising financial capital in its proper biblical place. We think financial capital is the ceiling when it's actually only the floor.

Stuffocation

This is a new word which we could easily add to our dictionary. The trend watcher James Wallmann coined the term 'stuffocation' to describe the feeling that too many things, too much stuff is suffocating our way of life.

Thanks to mass production and global markets, we have access to a huge amount of relatively cheap products which we readily buy ... and then store! The explosion of self-storage facilities over the past 10 years testifies to the fact that we have too much stuff and too little space to keep it. Not only too little physical space but also too little emotional space. The excess of things is beginning to show us that more is, in fact, less.

I was very surprised to read some comments from Steve Howard, Head of Sustainability at IKEA, a company which survives very nicely by offering us such a wide range of things we never knew we needed, who said "we have reached a limit on how much we can consume! We will be increasingly building a circular Ikea where you can repair and recycle products." In economic terms, Howard says, "If we look on a global basis, in the west we have probably hit peak stuff. We talk about peak oil. I'd say we've hit peak red meat, peak sugar, peak stuff ... peak home furnishings... "

We have reached a clutter crisis. The more we have, the more stress this brings. It all has to be managed, used, repaired, stored, maintained – and this is not bringing the satisfaction we expected!

So, what is the antidote for our disease called 'stuffocation'?

My suggestion is to start giving stuff away; after all it was Jesus

Himself who said "It is more blessed to give than to receive." Join in the 'sharing economy' in which things such as cars, mowers, tools could be shared with family and neighbours.

Downsizing can bring extra space in which to breathe … making your material life smaller can bring much needed space.

In the end, our life does not depend on how much stuff we can gather. The well-known bumper sticker "he who dies with the most toys wins' … doesn't ring true!

> Jesus told of a rich man who wanted to enjoy life, living off his accumulated assets. *"Take care, and be on your guard against all covetousness, for one's life does not consist in the abundance of his possessions[7]."*

And he told them a parable, saying, "The land of a rich man produced plentifully, and he thought to himself, 'What shall I do, for I have nowhere to store my crops?' And he said, 'I will do this: I will tear down my barns and build larger ones, and there I will store all my grain and my goods. And I will say to my soul, "Soul, you have ample goods laid up for many years; relax, eat, drink, be merry."' But God said to him, 'Fool! This night your soul is required of you, and the things you have prepared, whose will they be?' So is the one who lays up treasure for himself and is not rich toward God."

This week, think about some stuff you have which could be given away. Who could you make happy with it?

How Much Land Does a Man Need?

Leo Tolstoy tells this short story, 'How Much Land Does A Man Need?' of a greedy man named, *Pahom*, who was obsessed by amassing more and more land. One day he learned of a wonderful and unusual opportunity to get more land. For only 1,000 roubles he

---

7. Luke 12:15

could have the entire area that he could walk around in one day, but he had to make it back to the starting point by sunset or he would lose everything that he invested.

He arose early and set out. He walked on and on thinking that he could get just a little more land if he kept straining forward for the prize he sought, but he went so far that he realised he must walk very fast if he was going to get back to the starting point and claim the land. As the sun set lower in the sky, he quickened his pace. He began to run. He came within sight of the finishing goal and exerted his last energies plunging over the finish line, falling to the ground, dead.

His servant took a spade and dug a grave. He made it just long enough and just wide enough to match Pahom's body and buried him. Here's the title Tolstoy gave his story: *"How Much Land Does a Man Need?"* He ends this short story with this line: *"Six feet from his head to his heels was all that man needed".*

Contentment

Developing the discipline of contentment is essential in overcoming suffocation. Without this discipline, we will be given over to a lifestyle of more … more …

Contentment brings peace, rest, thankfulness and satisfaction - as we learn to trust in the Lord for our long-term goals. Contentment is not the fulfilment of our wants but the appreciation of what God has given us and the freedom to share these with others.

The writer of Hebrews answers the question, 'How much is enough?' The answer is, "Keep your lives free from the love of money and be content with what you have, because God has said, "Never will I leave you; never will I forsake you[8]." Enough is whatever I have right now. The resources currently at my disposal are enough. I don't need more of anything to answer any longing or need of my heart. I can be content with what I have because of the truth that God is with me, at

---

8. Hebrews 13:5

all times. His presence, not more resources, settles anxiety, insecurity, and dissatisfaction.

The apostle Paul gives a rich perspective to contentment. His experience in life had involved both plenty and lack, both self-sufficiency and dependency. Paul learned contentment as he experienced the indwelling power and strength of Christ. "I am not saying this because I am in need, for I have learned to be content whatever the circumstances. I know what it is to be in need, and I know what it is to have plenty. I have learned the secret of being content in any and every situation, whether well fed or hungry, whether living in plenty or in want. I can do all this through him who gives me strength[9]."

Paul applies contentment to both need and abundance. We tend to think more contentment is needed when we are struggling to live with less than what seems ideal to us. However, Paul's teaching lets us know that when we experience abundance, we also deeply need to practice contentment through the strength of Jesus so that we don't fall into it's unique traps. Learning to be content is for everyone, not just for those who experience lack!

I remember the great boxer Sonny Liston, pictured in a major fight wearing shorts carrying the verse, Philippians 4:13! Well, it may be true generally, but the phrase specifically referred to being content in any and all situations!

Let's contrast contentment and the lack of it.

A discontentment perspective expects that more of something external will solve internal struggles. A contentment perspective recognises that what I have right now is enough and that God's presence and power answers my struggles, fuelling my ability to be satisfied with my current circumstances.

---

9. Philippians 4:11-13

The problems with discontentment are:

Uncertainty - will I (ever) have enough?

Dissatisfaction - enjoyment disappears quickly

Greed - focus on material things, which the Bible calls idolatry

Jealousy - a focus on self-interest, which leads to independence and selfishness

Overconsumption - the pursuit of more, which leads to restlessness.

The goal of wealth

So what is the goal of wealth accumulation, which will arise from productive work? Listening to Andrew Carnegie in a 1889 article 'The goal of wealth' he sets out the duty of the man of wealth.

"First, to set an example of modest, unostentatious living, shunning display or extravagance; to provide moderately for the legitimate wants of those dependent upon him; and after doing so to consider all surplus revenues which come to him simply as trust funds, which he is called upon to administer."

Wealth creation is not merely the accumulation of money but should be seen in the ability to lead a good life. The goal of our work should be to build an asset-based economy in which the assets are managed for people to enjoy the God-given life. The focus should not be on money but on all the different types of assets needed for the good life. Examples are physical assets to enjoy good health; emotional assets to enjoy inner strength and peace; time assets with which to enjoy meaningful relationships; spiritual assets to enjoy Gods activity.

Financial assets are important, in a balanced relationship to the other forms of assets, with which we can be generous and achieve long term, life goals.

For the follower of Jesus, this means developing an eternal perspective on wealth creation. The 'good life' in which we find contentment and happiness is to be found in the ability to give, as he stated, "it is more blessed to give than to receive[10]." He founded the 'sharing economy' which characterized the early church.

"Now the full number of those who believed were of one heart and soul, and no one said that any of the things that belonged to him was his own, but they had everything in common. And with great power the apostles were giving their testimony to the resurrection of the Lord Jesus, and great grace was upon them all. There was not a needy person among them, for as many as were owners of lands or houses sold them and brought the proceeds of what was sold and laid it at the apostles' feet, and it was distributed to each as any had need[11]."

The Oxford Professor

'The £33,000 a year Oxford Don giving £1 million to African Aid!' This appeared in English newspapers in November 2009. What a life goal! I asked myself - how is this possible?

As an academic earning £33,000 a year, Toby Ord may seemed an unlikely candidate to give £1million to charity, but the Oxford University researcher has pledged to donate a large portion of his lifetime earnings to save lives in Africa.

The article explained, "He will sacrifice a big house, fast cars and foreign travel to give a large proportion of his salary to small charities working on the ground who buy drugs to treat those suffering from TB and tropical diseases! He is starting off by effectively reducing his annual salary to £20,000 – and giving the rest away."

Dr Ord calculates that, allowing for inflation and pay rises, he will be able to hit his £1million target. He estimates his salary from Oxford's Balliol College will average £42,000 over the remaining 35 years of

---

10. Acts 20:32
11. Acts 4:23,24

his career. The amount of his salary he keeps will also rise in line with inflation.

He said, "Many people agree that global poverty is one of the biggest moral problems of our time, but very few people are prepared to donate a large part of their income to help eliminate it. I decided to put my money where my mouth was and to set up a society for people who want to join me in this. Ideally it will become a well-recognised way of living one's life … I did all the calculations and realised I could save the lives of thousands.

Saving just one person's life is often thought to be an amazing kind of thing you can do over your whole career."

Dr Ord has launched a group, Giving What We Can, to encourage others to donate at least 10 per cent of their pre-tax income to the development aid charities of their choice. So far 23 people have signed up. The pledge is not legally binding but is designed as a lifetime commitment. The money is paid directly to the charities rather than going through his group. The pledge states: *'I recognise that I can use part of my income to do a significant amount of good in the developing world.*

"Since I can live well enough on a smaller income, I pledge that from today until the day I retire, I shall give at least 10 per cent of what I earn to whichever organisations can most effectively use it to fight poverty in the developing world."

After the start in 2009, the total donations from the community "Giving Wat We Can" totalled more than £7 million at the end of 2014. "In May 2015, we celebrated reaching over 1000 members, together pledging more than $400M. We now have 1,371 members, who have pledged to donate over $527 million over the course of their careers. We've also moved more than $10,466,826 through Giving What We Can Trust." The charity is still going strong! One couple decided to live on 'enough' for them, and to give the rest away - a wonderful example, which has been copied by many!

GENERATIONAL PLANNING VS SHORT-TERM RESULTS

In our private lives, our expenditure is largely determined by the idea, "I want it, and I want it now," which leads to impulse purchases and an increase in debt. A short-term mindset also undermines the shift toward sustainability, because consumption eats away at tomorrow. Of course, in the short-term we must manage our resources well and efficiently, but without the perspective of long-term impact, the focus will be on immediate results with no concern for future effects.

Shareholders demand quarterly earnings miracles. The pressure put on staff of larger corporations is very stressful. Too often what looks like 'success' today can inhibit a company's competitiveness tomorrow. Pressure to produce short-term results has increased in the last five years, according to 63 percent of global executives who responded to a recent McKinsey & Company survey. This has fostered what the business community has come to call 'short-termism,' defined by the Financial Times as "an excessive focus on short-term results at the expense of long-term interests."

God always thinks in generations and wants to bless us to the fourth generation! The problem is that we are now eating our children's legacy through our short-term thinking and increasing debt. Building wealth for future generations is a task for the Kingdom's economy. In the economy of the common kingdom, our horizon is so near to us that we are only thinking of short-term results. The pressure on profits in large companies is at the expense of relationships and continuity.

We must learn to think about the effects of our efforts far beyond our own lifetime (so-called 'cathedral thinking'). In whom can I invest, so that the work continues for the next generations? I'm fascinated by the builders of the pyramids. They had a vision so great that they knew that only their grandchildren would be there to enjoy the fruits of their efforts. As management thinker Charles Handy wrote, "Put your focus on immortality, or as close as you can get, and most ethical dilemmas will solve themselves. Today the skyscrapers of business tower over the old cathedrals. We must hope that those who build the towers of businesses are 'cathedral builders'. If they fail, we all fail."

An economist stated, "if you want to make money for a year you ask one set of questions, but if you want to make money for 100 years you ask different questions." The 100-year questions revolve around mutuality and sustainability and challenge the purely profit-driven approach to business rooted in Milton Friedman's short-term economic theory.

God's way of blessing is by the family. This is the defining unity in the economy of the kingdom of God. In the economy of the Old Testament land belongs to the family and would be handed down from generation to generation. "I will bless those who bless you, and those who curse you, I will curse; and in you all generations of the earth shall be blessed." (Genesis 12:3)

The Bible says clearly that wealth which has been gained quickly cannot be held for long. "An inheritance gained hastily in the beginning will not be blessed in the end[1]." "A faithful man will abound with blessings, but whoever hastens to be rich will not go unpunished.[2]" Why is this? Because the skill sets required to manage it correctly have not been developed. We hear very often about lottery winners who squander the money in a very short time. Professional athletes

---

1. Proverbs 20:21
2. Proverbs 28:20

who come from poverty into millions of euros and then retire only to be flat broke soon afterwards. Those people who are able to hold onto their riches and even increase them do this because the wisdom to manage them was passed on prior to that receiving their assets.

Multi-generational planning

"The righteous lead blameless lives; blessed are their children after them[3]."

The family is the primary unit of economics. In the Old Testament, property (land) belonged to the family and was passed from generation to generation. Fathers are to provide other forms of inheritance for their children[4]. A parent who fails to provide for his/her family is "worse than an unbeliever[5]." Thus, family economics, present and future, are intended to be intergenerational.

This centrality of the family is not to disparage the roles of single men and women in an economy, especially those who are called to singleness[6]. However, an individual is not a functioning unit, as the family in which there is a head, a wife and children. There are mutual roles within the family of education, training, and provision. Even as one generation lives their lives as God's stewards on earth, they are making provision for the next. A major weakness of Christians and churches on their culture has been the loss of belief from one generation to the next. This loss is not part of God's preceptive design.

I find it striking that when Keynes, the founder of modern capitalism, was asked about the long-term consequences of 'taxed and spend' policies, he replied, 'Well, in the long run we're all dead.'

Writer Denis Peacocke says that if you don't pay attention to future generations, if you don't love your children, the economy will be

---

3. Proverbs 20:7
4. Proverbs 13:22
5. I Timothy 5:8
6. I Corinthians 7:6-8

characterised by debt and consumption. We'll eat our children's wealth, their heritage, today! The curse of poverty is 'one-generation wealth,' which is not passed on to our children but consumed, exacerbated by inheritance tax and anti-family policies.

Gods pipeline for blessing is the family unit. God's covenant with Abraham is described as, "Abraham will surely become a great and powerful nation, and all nations on earth will be blessed through him. For I have chosen him, so that he will direct his children and his household after him to keep the way of the Lord by doing what is right and just, so that the Lord will bring about for Abraham what he has promised him[7]."

During the time of exile in Babylon, the people are encouraged to contribute to the local economy. "Build houses and settle down; plant gardens and eat what they produce. Marry and have sons and daughters; find wives for your sons and give your daughters in marriage, so that they too may have sons and daughters. Increase in number there; do not decrease[8]." People coming along with the next generation are essential for a well-functioning economy.

In his very helpful book "Doing Business God's way", Dennis Peacock introduces the concept of Christians being involved in what he calls a new family enterprise called Almightily and Co. We are born again into a relationship with God as our Father and with fellow Christians as brothers and sisters who are being apprenticed into running the family business. That apprenticeship is about responsibility, stewardship, and buying in to God's work and people.

God is a God of generations. We need an economy that strongly supports the formation and enhancement of nuclear family structures as the primary social group within society. The economic momentum of families across the generations is a critical element in God's plan to bless the nations.

---

7. Genesis 18:18,19
8. Jeremiah 29:5,6

Paul writes that children are not responsible to save up for their parents, but parents for their children[9].   Our children are as stewardship, heritage, and an inheritance from the Lord[10]. God requires us to pass on our wealth to them and to raise them in the faith as we teach them to choose the moral principles of Scripture.

Generational momentum is like a relay race since the previous generations pass on to future generations the baton of their wealth, knowledge, spiritual insights and stewardship skills so that every succeeding generation is starting off at the success levels of their predecessors.

I think it is important here to make a distinction between wealth and riches. Riches can be defined as perishable assets which Christ warns us not to improperly focus upon as the primary goal of our labours. He called these 'treasures on earth.' He also warned us never to love them. "Since you trust in your deeds and in riches, you too will be taken captive[11]…"   Riches are a product of the money which you employ to work for you. Wealth on the other hand is primarily achieved through the application of skills, spiritual knowledge, and character developed in obeying God's ways of approaching resource management. Riches are something we have; wealth is something we are. Wealth is internal, riches are external.

I do not come from a family which has been blessed with great riches. However, I do come from a family blessed with great wealth.

My grandfather passed on to his daughter, my mother, some aspects of this great wealth which have then been passed on to me. Material wealth was defined by a sense of deep contentment in having enough, a financial wealth which enables us to always being in a position to bless others and emotional wealth which taught us to be able to cope with any circumstances and to love others in spite of what they may do to us, And a spiritual wealth which enabled us to get to know God

---

9. 2 Corinthians 12:14
10. Psalm 127
11. Jeremiah 48:7

and to enjoy his daily presence.

Economic cost of abortion

In 2008, there were over 1.2 million unborn children murdered by abortionists in the United States. In many nations we see very high rates of abortion. These babies, unlike those who chose to abort hem, had no 'choice' and they would probably rather NOT have died. I wonder if the social liberal pro-abortion types have considered all of the consequences of taking away so many lives from this nation – over 52 million lives lost since 1973!

Admittedly, it is a rather cold, callous path of logic to analyse abortion in terms of economics, but let's go there for a few moments. Back in 1998, the late Larry Burkett, a highly regarded author on Christian personal financial topics wrote 'The George Bailey Effect: Abortion-on-Demand and the Implications for America's Economic Future.' Burkett examined abortion not from the moral perspective, but its impact on the economics of the United States. He makes a profound point. The growing parity between the old and the young is at the heart of the demographic challenges that face Medicare and Social Security. Incredible as it may seem, by the time the peak of the baby boom generation reaches retirement age, the number of abortions since the Supreme Court's Roe v. Wade decision will equal the number of births in the baby boom. "If only one-third of those who have been aborted were available to start work on their 18th birthday," speculated USA Today, "the demise of Social Security would be put off for decades."

Indeed, it is largely because of abortion-on-demand that by the year 2030 the ratio of workers to Social Security beneficiaries will be reduced to the only 2-to-1, according to a projection from the Social Security Board of Trustees. In other words, two workers will be supporting one retiree. When the program began in the 1930s, 42 workers supported each retiree.

The murder of millions of babies since Roe v Wade has had a profound impact on the demographics of the United States. As a result of removing that staggering number of lives, the population – and its tax base – is far smaller. If we assume a fairly steady rate of abortions since that year of reporting (2008), then there have been almost 56M aborted babies in this country – nearly the population of California and Texas combined. Given an average federal tax revenue of approximately $8500 per citizen, and assuming that those aborted between 1975 and 1990 (approximately 23,782,000 lives) would now be productive taxpayers and the U.S. economy is losing roughly $202 billion per year in tax payments as of 2012.

Sustainability

The kingdom's economy is looking for sustainability to preserve resources for future generations.

God created people to exercise dominion, to be fruitful and multiply, to receive God's provision, to work in relationships, and to observe the limits of creation. We noted that these have often been called the "creation mandate" or "cultural mandate," which is expressed as follows.

"God blessed them, and God said to them, 'Be fruitful and multiply, and fill the earth and subdue it; and have dominion over the fish of the sea and over the birds of the air and over every living thing that moves upon the earth[12].'" "The Lord God took the man and put him in the garden of Eden to till it and keep it[13]."

The first phrase "be fruitful and multiply," means to develop the social world: build families, churches, schools, cities, governments, laws. The second phrase, "subdue the earth," means to harness the natural world: plant crops, build bridges, design computers, and compose music.

Sustainability starts with Gods creation - natural capital, which we must look after for the next generation and not consume with a lack

---

12. Genesis 1:28
13. Genesis 2:15

of regard for the future. The same applies to people - human capital. We should nurture and train the next generations. When well-trained people, working together in harmony, use their productive capital to develop and sustain the natural capital, then financial capital will follow. Focus on financial capital first, then people will be used and mis-used, followed by wastefulness of our natural capital.

Some time ago, I met with some Dutch Christian businessmen in a very stately home on the Herengracht in Amsterdam. Our host was Ernst van Eeghen, at that time, the CEO of the family business, which was founded in 1662, during the Dutch 'Golden Age' by Jacob van Eeghen in Amsterdam. Jacob fled as a Huguenot Protestant to Amsterdam from Antwerp, Belgium as a refugee from the Spanish domination in that country. The company's products included: linen, linseed, wool, wine, timber, salt and sugar, first focussing on Europe and later the West Indies. The company was a competitor of the monopolistic Dutch East India company, the VOC, which incidentally was the very first public company to be traded on the Amsterdam stock exchange.

The walls of their offices are decorated with paintings of ancestors from the VOC era. For over 350 years, the business has remained in the family. Continuity and not profit maximisation is for Van Eeghen the most important goal of the company. One aim of the company is that family members should not take over an executive role until they have spent at least 7 years in another business outside of Holland, so that they have the right kind of practical experience prior to being trained in-company.

Sustainability requires a long-term perspective. It also requires an attitude of a current advantage in order to obtain something better in the future!

Research[14] conducted by the IMD Group, identified four major clusters in which family businesses have over centuries, been high

---

14. *https://www.imd.org/research-knowledge/articles/secrets-of-success-in-long-lasting-family-firms*

performing. They are:

Long-term success in the business. The principles in this category are Vision, Entrepreneurial Drive, Business Skills, Employees, Ethics, Succession Process and Adaptability.

Long-term continuity of the family. The identified principles in this category are: Pride, Mutual Support, Strong Values, Social Engagement, Fairness, Ability to Handle Conflict, and Strength in Unity.

Long-term success in ownership. The key principles in this category are: Trust, Control, the Equal/Unequal concept, Voting Rights, Responsible Ownership and Equity Concentration.

Success in innovation. The fourth dimension of attributes relates to how high-performing family firms distinguish and renew themselves. The five key areas are: Separation of Issues, Formal Processes, Stewardship, Governance Structures and Role of the Family.

Without a long-term perspective, businesses will die. Remember airlines like Pan-Am and Eastern, Kodak, top accounting firm Arthur Anderson, Woolworth's, telecom giant WorldCom, investment bank Lehman Brothers?

Investing in people

We need to invest in people, so that my business can be taken over by someone else ... (not necessarily my kids) ... this is discipleship ... multiplying yourself, your ideas, vision, your skills.

One of my favourite TV shows is 'Dragon's Den', or in the US it is called, 'The Shark Tank.' In it, entrepreneurs with good ideas, or new businesses seek investment from investors who not only invest their money, but also their time in coaching, opening networks etc. One big lesson which can be learned from those people who won an investment, is that investors invest in people, not things. However good the idea or business proposition may be, if the person is not seemed to be trustworthy, or if there is no 'click,' then no investment will be won.

It's the people who make the company. The employer-employee relationship in a working industry is a mutual bond. The employers are there to manage and supervise the employees, while the employees are there to accomplish all the tasks required to make the company keep advancing. If the employers are the mind and soul, the employees are the heart and body of the industry. Companies should invest in motivating their workers to boost productivity which, in turn, makes the company grow.

The best investment you can make in life is to invest in people. The highlight of discussions these days among businesspeople is investing in the stock market where they debate on the best stock to invest. Nevertheless, the best investment we can make is to invest in people. Jesus did this by giving His time, His energy, His love, and His support to people.

Investing in human capital can mean providing funds for a person's education, training, and even medical care to make him/her be more productive at work. An employee with outstanding performance in the company is always an asset!

In my last business as CEO of a space services company, I remember evaluating our tenders for contracts we won at the European Space Agency, together with their head of contracts. She said that a major factor behind the reason we got the contracts was we had the best people and the best plan for training them.

ABUNDANCE VS SCARCITY

One of the fundamental principles of economy is the allocation of scarce resources. Whether it is too little time, money, food, social contacts or anything else: scarcity influences our choices and behaviour. The French philosopher Jean-Paul Sartre, in his book 'The Critique of Dialectical Reason', observes that scarcity is the overriding rule of life and concluded that the fundamental issue of human existence is scarcity when you examine it from a purely physical realm. As Christians, we do not look at life from a purely physical realm.

Steven Covey wrote in his book, "Seven Habits of Highly Effective People, "Most people are deeply scripted in what I call the Scarcity Mentality. They see life as having only so much, as though there was only one pie out there. And if someone were to get a big piece of the pie, it would mean less for everybody else. Most people operate with the Scarcity Mentality — meaning they act as though everything is zero-sum (in other words, if you get it, I don't). People with the Scarcity Mentality have a very hard time-sharing recognition or credit and find it difficult to be genuinely happy about other people's successes."

God does not know scarcity at all. He is a creator and is carrying on with his creative work and invites us to join him in his work. The Bible starts out with a liturgy of abundance. Genesis 1 is a song of praise for God's generosity.

The Bible reminds us that God is Lord of all the earth. He is not limited to our so-called scarce resources. "God is able to abundantly bless you with all his grace, so that at any time and in every way you will have sufficient for yourself and also be able to contribute to the needs of others and every good work[1]." Notice how many times the words 'all, every' occur to signify the stability of His promise of provision. Notice also the threefold purpose of abundance - enough for daily living, to be generous and do good work.

Scarcity often leads to human ingenuity and creativity … our task is to set this free, to encourage innovation. Economics has been concerned with allocating scarce resources …. There is only one apple … how do you allocate this? But what if we come along with a better way of growing more apples? God's economy is more concerned with creativity and productivity with which we can alleviate poverty.

The belief in scarcity--that leads to a misunderstanding of the process of creating wealth. A society's wealth is determined not by the supply of physical resources, which are supposedly limited, but by human ingenuity, which constantly redefines what counts as a resource in the first place. In the nineteenth century, as the supply of whale blubber shrank, humankind found a way to make use of the worthless black goo that oozed out of the ground in Texas and the natural gas that was regarded as a hazard in Pennsylvania coal mines. Today, the most important technology, the microchip, is made out of the world's most common material--silicon, which is basically sand. So, wealth is not limited by physical resources, it is as unlimited as the power of our minds.

Julian Simon, the author of a 1981 book called, 'The Ultimate Resource' described how six commodities thought to be running out … 10 years later – all had increased.

Many people believe that global population growth leads to exhaustion of our resources, greater poverty and more famines, but evidence suggests otherwise. Between 1960 and 2016, the world's population

---

1. 2 Corinthians 9:7

increased by 145 percent. Over the same time period, real average annual per capita income in the world rose by 183 percent. In 1981, the World Bank estimated, 42.2 percent of humanity lived on less than $1.90 per person per day (adjusted for purchasing power). In 2013, that figure stood at 10.7 percent.

In his book, Simon noted that, "Humans are intelligent animals who innovate their way out of scarcity through greater efficiency, increased supply, or development of substitutes. Human ingenuity, in other words, is 'the ultimate resource' that makes other resources more plentiful."

Creativity is a God-given talent, not only in the Kingdom of God but also in the common kingdom. We all need to develop this God-given gift of creativity. A 'scarcity mentality' causes tunnel vision, hinders learning, and misses out on the possibility to experience co-creating with God, as we trust Him to inspire us to harness His creative power. Our view of God has its focus on the three-person God of Love, whose creative energy made everything from nothing at all by his Word.

Economics as Choice

One Biblical supposition affecting our view of the economy is that God created man knowing he would have basic needs, such as food, clothing, and shelter. God created everything that was needed to meet those needs. God created natural resources and renewable resources (through photosynthesis and reproduction). We can have confidence that God has provided all that we need; thus, we can have faith to seek, find, and process abundant natural resources.

We do not live in a resource short world. If we follow God's ways and continue to seek for new ideas and new ways to look at the resources He has put in the earth, we will always have that which is needed to have life abundantly and to take dominion over the earth.

While God has created the earth such that we have renewable resources, resources must be well managed and utilised. We must use the resources we have in a frugal manner in order to gain the greatest benefit from them. We are to be good stewards of all the things God has given to us.

It is true that some resources are limited, and we must manage limited resources judiciously, implying we must make wise choices. Thus, economics can be called the science of choice. In the broad sense, economics is the study of the choices men make to better their households. Economics is unique to man because only man can choose. Man can choose, because he was created in the image of God with the ability to choose. God can choose, and so can man. This choice is what makes anything valuable. If God declares something has value, then it does. His choice makes it valuable. Likewise, man's choice gives value to things. "Value exists only in the mind, that is, all value is determined by man, who arranges things or available choices according to his own unique scale of preference or value."

However, we often choose differently than God would, and this has consequences. For example, some people do not value human life and have killed many people. Some men have placed great value on immoral things, contrary to what God says. Some will misuse and waste natural resources. Christians will choose to use the God-given resources responsibly.

The value of material things is determined by the value man places upon them, by how he thinks about them. What he thinks is affected by his worldview and also his circumstances. Consider for example what is more valuable, water or diamonds. Most men place a much greater value upon diamonds than water (due to the relative abundance of each) and would exchange a huge volume of water for one diamond, if the owner of a diamond would agree to this. But in certain circumstances, for example for one lost in a desert, water becomes much more valuable than a cup full of diamonds. The relative availability of something affects how men value a thing in their mind, but this is not the only factor.

An item may be scarce (like a modern pop-art painting), but many people would assign no value to it. Value is imputed to something by the choice that individuals make based upon their own scale value. Some people would pay millions for some modern abstract paintings; I would pay nothing, or little, and that only considering I could sell it to someone with a completely different value base. Some would pay lots of money to see certain musicians in concert that I would not go to see unless someone paid me.

God wants us to make choices which benefit mankind and advance God's Kingdom. Our material choices flow from our spiritual and moral beliefs. Moral and ethical concerns are intertwined with economic choices. In fact, the founder of modern economics, Adam Smith, was the instructor of moral philosophy at the University of Glasgow; and his book 'The Wealth of Nations,' (1776) was developed out of his prior book, 'The Theory of Moral Sentiments' (1759).

Provision

The children of Israel left Egypt, the land of scarcity, thinking they would bounce into the land of abundance. Instead, they find themselves at risk in a wilderness, a desert with no visible life-support systems, a place of even greater scarcity where even bread seemed an impossibility. Having inhaled the continuing reality of scarcity throughout their lives, the Israelites start to breathe out murmurs, complaints, condemnations, and remembering 'the flesh pots of Egypt.'

Then, in this desert wilderness, bread inexplicably appears. A fine, flaky substance comes down. The Hebrews exclaimed, *"Manhue?"* -- Hebrew for "What is it?" -- and the word "manna" was born. They had never before received bread as a free gift that they couldn't control, predict, plan for or own. Gifts of life are given by a generous God. It's a wonder, it's a miracle, it's an embarrassment, it's irrational, but God's abundance transcends the market economy.

Three things happened to this bread in Exodus 16. First, everybody had enough. But because Israel had learned to believe in scarcity in Egypt, people started to hoard the bread. When they tried to bank it, to invest it, it turned sour and rotted, because you cannot store up God's generosity. Finally, Moses said, "You know what we ought to do? We ought to do what God did in Genesis I. We ought to have a Sabbath." Sabbath means that there's enough bread, that we need to stop working and thank God for His provision. That we don't need to worry about not working because on the day before, He gives a double portion!

This experience overturns their conviction about scarcity and cancels their anxiety about hunger. The gift of bread transforms the wilderness. And from that point on, Israel would entertain the thought that a place of perceived scarcity may turn out to be a place of wondrous abundance. Jesus said, "I am the bread of life, whoever comes to me shall not hunger[2]."

Multiplication

The economy of the kingdom is characterised by multiplication. Consider the parable of the sower, whereby the seed, when the conditions are good, increases 100-fold. The farmer would be very disappointed if he only got a good 10% return on his efforts!

Our investment of money in the common kingdom is rewarded with a small percentage increase, if we do it well, but we always have a notion that it should be more. This is the reason why we gamble and speculate, even turn to crime. Only that which is invested in what God has created and blessed will be able to be multiplied, like ideas, influence, products, people, righteousness, and yes even money, provided that this is invested in the kingdom of God.

The disciples of Jesus realised they had a serious budget deficit when asked by Jesus to feed the 5'000. When the small boy donated his lunch of bread and fish, Kingdom economics started to work and the investment was multiplied. "Jesus gave thanks and broke the loaves. Then he gave them to the disciples, and the disciples gave them to

---

2. John 6:35

the people.[3]"

When did the multiplication of the loaves and fish to feed the hungry multitudes of people that Jesus was healing occur? Was it in the blessing, the breaking, or the distribution by the disciples that the miracle of provision showed up? If the multiplication came in the blessing of Jesus, then a pile as big as a haystack would have appeared on the ground. If it was in the breaking, Jesus would have been breaking off bread and fish into baskets for a couple hours to feed 7,000 or 8,000 people. The text never says that happened. It appears it was in the distribution by the disciples -- the food just never ran out, similar to the oil and flour that lasted through a famine in the Old Testament. When Jesus blesses, your efforts are multiplied.

Walter Bruegemann stated, "In feeding the hungry crowd, Jesus reminds us that the wounds of scarcity can be healed only by faith in God's promise of abundance."

Only what God has created and blessed will He multiply. These include ideas, influence, products, customers, people, righteousness.

Poverty

Jesus said "the poor you will always have with you" ... but He takes poverty out of people, not only people out of poverty. To become free of an internal poverty of spirit, I must first remove it internally. Jesus takes poverty out of people as a priority!

Poverty is a spiritual problem, just like materialism. An inner infirmity of soul and spirit that manifests itself in the outer world by a scarcity of resources. Poverty is the fruit of sin, both collectively (parental, social, national) and individually. Poverty is not cured merely by changing circumstances. Man wants to blame his environment for poverty.

Naturally, we with resources have a responsibility to help alleviate

---

3. Mark 6:42

poverty; first of all by imparting skills and creating opportunities, not by giving money. Money cannot cure an internal spiritual state. We need to inspire people to creativity, create opportunities to improve their situations, and help them discover and use the resources God has already given them.

We can help alleviate poverty by creating chances for meaningful work, offer interest-free capital loans for entrepreneurs, teach skills and communicate God's message of provision.

The Bible tells of a widow, whose husband, a leading prophet, died and left her with debts she couldn't pay. When crying out to the prophet Elisha, the first question she received as a start to getting out of poverty was "what do you have?" Of course, she answered 'Nothing." A logical answer as that was her problem! However, in Gods economy, she is asked to put what she has in God's hands and develop it! You can read this story in 2 Kings 4:1-7. What did she have which she did not count on? Well, she had the help of her children, a trusted network of neighbours, Elisha's help, God's supernatural help and her marketing skills!

When placed in God's hands, when transferred into God's economy, a little can be multiplied. Jesus says, as it were, "Put the resources in my hand and see what I can do with it." Scarcity becomes abundance.

Economics defying generosity

A characteristic of the church's distinctive ethic is its generosity which transcends scarcity.

One of the basic teachings we learn at college about economics is that it is the allocation of scarce resources. There is only so much to go around, a piece of property cannot be enjoyed by everyone. A certain sum of money can only satisfy a limited number of desires.

The economics defying principles of the Kingdom transcend the complex theories of our world's economists. A poor widow who gives her last two small copper coins, all she has heft, is said to have offered more than all the rich combined. In the Corinthian church, their 'extreme poverty' overflows into a 'wealth of generosity' that turns out to be an 'abundance' which richly supplies the needs of others[4]!

By worldly standards these Corinthians would seem to lack 'financial responsibility' in being cheerfully generous 'beyond their means[5].'

When analysed by economic rules, this seems to be irrational. In God's economy this abundance does not come out of nothing, but out of the work of God in multiplying that which we put into His hands. He is 'able to make all grace abound to you, so that at all times, having everything you need, you may abound in every good work[6].' When the impoverished give generously, God makes them 'enriched' in their experience[7].

This seemingly irresponsible generosity makes everyone spiritually richer in ways that economists can never calculate. "This service that you perform is not only supplying the needs of the Lord's people but is also overflowing in many expressions of thanks to God.

Because of the service by which you have proved yourselves, others will praise God for the obedience that accompanies your confession of the gospel of Christ, and for your generosity in sharing with them and with everyone else. And in their prayers for you, their hearts will go out to you, because of the surpassing grace God has given you[8]."

The God who owns the cattle on a thousand hills[9] and the gold in every mine[10] can easily defy the laws of economics!

---

4. 2 Corinthians 8:2,14
5. 2 Corinthians 8:3 and 9:7
6. 2 Corinthians 9:8
7. 2 Corinthians 9:11
8. 2 Corinthians 9:12-14
9. Psalm 50:10
10. Haggai 2:8

Corruption - a major cause of poverty

Corruption delays, distorts and diverts economic growth. It's a serious issue for business because corruption increases the risks and decreases returns on investments. But above all, it has a devastating impact on ordinary people who have to live in a country where corruption is rife. It means they can't get the goods and services they should be able to without paying bribes and it means the resources in their country may be expropriated to other parts of the world by corrupt elites. It devastates lives.

The big C of corruption can be countered by four more C's!

The first is the sense of 'connectedness'. A lack of connectedness or belongingness breeds corruption in society. Often you see people looking for connections in order to avoid corruption! Corruption is much more in urban areas because there is no community sense there. A sense of belongingness among people can root out corruption.

The second C is 'courage'. A lack of self-esteem or confidence in one's ability, fear or insecurity in a person makes one become more corrupt. He then tries to find his security only through money. But the more money he acquires, the more afraid and fearful he becomes because the money is not earned in a right manner.

The third C is 'care' and 'compassion'. Care and compassion in society can bring dedication to the wellbeing of others. This means having the sense that somebody has a greater need than myself.

The last C is a sense of 'commitment' — commitment to contribution. When a person has a commitment to a higher cause in life, it brings a shift from getting to giving. In society, if everyone keeps thinking, 'What can I gain?' rather than 'What can I contribute', then corruption cannot be rooted out.

All this is not possible without spiritual upliftment and a sense of belongingness with the world. Our world has become a village. We have globalised everything but wisdom. This is one of the causes of terrorism and unrest. We accept food from every part of the world, music from every part of the world, but when it comes to wisdom, people seem to shy away.

Pope-onomics

Pope Francis, known for his more liberal views than his predecessors, spoke at the US Congress. His address made Speaker John Boehner cry … The Pope described the core of his teaching, which Time magazine dubbed 'Pope-onomics.'

"It goes without saying that part of this great effort is the creation and distribution of wealth. The right use of natural resources, the proper application of technology and the harnessing of the spirit of enterprise are essential elements of an economy, which seeks to be modern, inclusive and sustainable."

He spoke against liberal economics, making a good case for reducing income inequality and providing for the poor.

"Jesus tells us that it is the 'protocol' on the basis of which we will be judged, it is what we read in Chapter 25 of Matthew: "I had hunger, I had thirst, I was in prison, I was sick, I was naked and you helped me: dressed me, visited me, you took care of me," the pontiff continued.

"Every time that we do this to our brother, we do this to Jesus. To have care of our neighbour: who is poor, who suffers in the spirit, who is in need. This is the touchstone, it is the Gospel."

"The Gospel message is a message open to all," the pope continues. "The Gospel does not condemn the rich but idolatry of wealth, that idolatry that renders [us] insensitive to the cries of the poor."

In this interview, he was asked if the progress of capitalism over the past decennia was irreversible. Pope Francis answered," I recognise that globalisation has helped many people to rise from poverty, but it has condemned many others to hunger. It's true that in absolute terms it grows world wealth, but it also increased the disparity and the new kinds of poverty. What I notice is that this system is maintained with the culture of waste, of which I have already spoken several times. There is a politics, sociology, and also an attitude of rejection.

When at the centre of the system there is not anymore man but money, when money becomes an idol, men and women are reduced and simply instruments of a social system and an economy characterised, indeed dominated by deep imbalances.

Who else but committed Christians can clean up the economy? Where are the Church leaders who speak out on our economy?"

ETERNAL REWARDS VS TEMPORAL GAIN

Someone asked God, "What do you notice about mankind?" God replied, "That they lose their health in order to gain money, and then lose their money in order to regain their health. That, by fearfully thinking about the future, they forget the present, so that they live neither for the present nor for the future. That they live as if they will never die, and that they die as if they have never lived!"

Eternity begins today, and we must remember that everything we do today is just a preparation for eternity. Maturity can be described as denying yourself something today in order to obtain something better in the future. After all, that is the basis of investing and saving! Developing an eternal perspective is so important. The better our perspective on the future, the better and more informed will be our decisions today. If I know what the market for my products or service will be like in 3-5 years' time, then I can make plans to ensure I will be ready to make the most of the situation at that time. When we die, we will spend an eternity with the Lord, so what preparations am I making today?

The French philosopher, Teilhard de Chardin said, "We think we are in the land of the living on our way to the land of the dead. It's not like that! We are in the land of the dying on our way to the land of the living!" Eternity begins today and this has to determine our economic decisions as believers!

We have been designed for eternity. Solomon wrote, "He has made everything beautiful in its time. Also, he has put eternity into man's heart, yet so that he cannot find out what God has done from the beginning to the end[1]."

Madonna sang about our society... 'we are living in a a material world and I am a material girl.' In a materialistic world, eternity fades... after all, we live for the present and we often hear, "I want it, and I want it now!"

One day everyone will have to appear before Christ, who will ask us to account for what we have done with the power and the time and talents he has given us. "For we must all appear before the judgment seat of Christ, so that each one of us may receive what he deserves for what he has done in his life, whether it be good or bad[2]. This should motivate us to start focusing on God's economy and to use the resources entrusted to us in a responsible manner, as God wants us to do!

When Jesus spoke to a very rich young man, he gave an unexpected answer to the question, "Master, what must I do to inherit eternal life?" The young man was exemplary in keeping the law, but one thing was missing!

"Jesus said to him, 'If you want to be perfect, go and sell your property and give it to the poor, and you will have a treasure in heaven, and come here, follow me[3].'"

During the Sermon on the Mount Jesus urged listeners, "Do not lay up for yourselves treasures on earth, where moth and rust destroy and where thieves break in and steal, but lay up for yourselves treasures in heaven, where neither moth nor rust destroys and where thieves do not break in and steal. For where your treasure is, there your heart

---

1. Ecclesiastes 3:11
2. 2 Corinthians 5:10
3. Luke 8:18-30

will be also.[4]."

Treasures here on earth are very temporary and subject to decay; televisions break down or become obsolete quickly, cars lose their value quickly, jewellery and art can be stolen, printing money and inflation reduce the value of money and violence can destroy entire cities and countries.

Building up treasures in heaven is important because it determines our heart's condition!

Paul thanked the believers from Philippi for their gifts and said, "Not that I seek the gift, but I seek the fruit that increases in your account[5]." Could it indeed be that investing in 'treasures in heaven' opens a kind of account from where we can then 'reap rewards'?

A treasure in heaven - that is all which is placed in God's economy. When we limit our expenses by making a budget in prayer and out of faith; when we use money to help the poor, widows, orphans, and oppressed; when we invest money in projects for God's Kingdom, we build up treasures in heaven.

The fruit of the 'treasures in heaven' has two dimensions. First of all, the many rewards that are described in the Bible and await us as we enter into eternity with Jesus. But also today's fruit, such as an intimate relationship with Christ, the fruit of the Spirit and the provision of daily needs that Jesus spoke about when he said, "But first seek the Kingdom of God and His righteousness, and all these things will be given to you[6]."

Living in God's economy is focusing on the things that are above not that are on the earth[7]. It is first and foremost a focus of the heart.

Randy Alcorn stated, "All of life is a treasure hunt ... for a perfect

---

4. Matthew 6:19-21
5. Philippians 4:19
6. Matthew 6:33
7. Colossians 3:2

person in a perfect place." Our ultimate destiny is to become like Jesus, in our unique characters, and fellowship with Him forever. Should we then not be living predominantly for eternity and is not our life here a very important workplace in which we prepare to meet this perfect person in that perfect place?

Problems with short-term thinking

Short-term thinking creates long-term problems. In a November 2018 article in the Sydney Herald, researcher Ralph Ashton interviewed around a thousand Australian leading figures. He wrote, "I asked three questions. Is there really a problem with short-termism in Australia? The response was a unanimous yes. Is this problem any different from other times in Australia's 230-year history? Yes, again. It's the worst in living memory. What can be done about it? Only 2 per cent of the leaders I spoke to had concrete suggestions. You read that right: only about 20 of the 1000 leaders had tangible ideas."

As adults, we learn that we can put certain things off, only so long before the negative consequences start to outweigh the benefits. Short term thinking simply means considering only what is in front of you. Instead of considering the possible impacts of a course of action over the long term, we think about what might happen today, tomorrow or next week. Sometimes we get away with this, and we simply need to act to fix a problem or take an opportunity now. The real issue occurs when the consequences of our actions (or inaction) lie hidden, and only emerge over the longer term.

There is a passage from 'The Player,' a book by the Russian writer Fyodor Dostoevsky, which illustrates a key problem in dealing with money. Aleksej plays with high stakes on the roulette table for the poor but equally lovely Polina. But in the course of the evening, the desire for money wins out over his love. He loses Polina. Dostoevsky believed that there was a fundamental mistake in the nature of the Russians that prevented his country from cooperating well with Europe. This lack of cooperation was expressed at the table. "Roulette is simply made for the Russians," said Aleksej, the protagonist, and he told how easy it is to seduce Russians into ideas and into 'who can make them rich within two hours without having to work'. Aleksej continues: 'I would rather spend my whole life in a nomad tent in Kyrgyzstan... than to worship the German ideal". (By this he meant to serve the western way of money by doing honest work.)

This passage from 'The Player' illustrates an important economic principle. The shorter the time horizon of a community, the less chance of economic success. Those communities that cannot set goals for the future spend everything immediately, save nothing, have no eye for the future and pay attention to build up capital for future generations.

Delayed gratification

This is the ability to forego spending something today, in order to build up savings for the future. In the 1960's, a Stanford professor named Walter Mischel began conducting a series of important psychological studies.

During his experiments, Mischel and his team tested hundreds of children — most of them around the ages of 4 and 5 years old — and revealed what is now believed to be one of the most important characteristics for success in health, work, and life. The children who were willing to delay gratification and waited to receive the second marshmallow ended up having higher SAT scores, lower levels of substance abuse, lower likelihood of obesity, better responses to stress, better social skills as reported by their parents, and generally better scores in a range of other life measures.

The researchers followed each child for more than 40 years and over and over again, the group who waited patiently for the second marshmallow succeeded in whatever capacity they were measuring. In other words, this series of experiments proved that the ability to delay gratification was critical for success in life.

In the financial world, the rough equivalent of the Marshmallow test was conducted by the McKinsey Global Institute (MGI), the research arm of consulting firm McKinsey & Co. MGI studied 615 publicly traded companies, to see if those that resisted the pressure to focus on short-term financial results performed better over the long haul. MGI approached the study by devising a measurement, to capture the span of a company's focus.

The study which covered the time span of 2001 to 2015, discovered that those with long-term focus had, on average, 36 percent greater earnings growth than other companies, as well as higher revenue, market capitalisation and profits. Those companies also had economic superiority: They created 11,600 more jobs, on average, during the period than did the shorter-term-focused enterprises. And even though long-term-focused companies were hit harder than their shorter-term counterparts during the 2008–'09 financial crisis, they recovered more quickly.

> Let's look at two major reasons we get trapped into short-term thinking.

> Firstly, we undervalue future rewards. *The closer a reward is to the present moment in time, the more we value it.* The further away the reward is, the less value we place on it.

> Secondly, our culture encourages short-term thinking. Most companies are trying to maximize their profit, and they're going to present their product or service to us in the best light possible relative to this goal.

Short-term thinking is a major problem, but we can train ourselves to embrace long-term thinking in its place. It seems as though our brains were hard-wired to think short-term, as Darwinists would have us believe, for our survival. Harvard University psychology professor Daniel Gilbert stated, "The brain and the eye may have a contractual relationship in which the brain has agreed to believe what the eye sees, but in return the eye has agreed to look for what the brain wants." The spirit of God can change this. We were created with a sense of the eternal, that this world is 'not all there is.'

Larry Fink, the CEO of the global investment company, BlackRock

Inc., criticised companies for their intense focus on short-term quarterly profits which drive the wrong decisions for employees, customers, and the communities where they and their business partners operate around the world. BlackRock manages $6.3 trillion in assets for their clients.

He stated in his 2018 Letter to CEOs, "Society is demanding that companies, both public and private, serve a social purpose. To prosper over time, every company must not only deliver financial performance, but also show how it makes a positive contribution to society. Companies must benefit all of their stakeholders, including shareholders, employees, customers, and the communities in which they operate."

In our economy, we need to maximise and promote the lifetime value of products. Most fashion, technology, and consumer-goods companies deliberately shorten the lives of their products. As the design expert Peter Fiell says: "Designers fail when they act irresponsibly at a time when we need to make less of everything and make products last longer." In austere times, there is an opportunity to promote the long-term value–let's call it the price per year of a product.

Creating products that endure and maybe even become more valuable as they age, as well as finding new ways of doing business that would make such a model profitable, is an innovation challenge worth pursuing for long-term-thinking entrepreneurs and designers. The "cradle to grave" philosophy of product responsibility has evolved into a "cradle to cradle" philosophy. Designers must now consider each stage of a product's lifecycle, which ranges from the design and manufacturing stages to the end-of-life stage, and includes reuse, recycling, and disposal. This requires long-term thinking.

Short term thinking has given rise to concerns about pollution, global warming and the depletion of natural resources and have persuaded many to conserve and recycle, not waste. We need an ethic of consumption.

The three "Rs" of managing waste are "reduce, reuse and recycle." A Christian ethic of consumption would address recycling as a spiritual expression of solidarity with creation and the rest of the world. The energy saved from recycling one glass bottle is enough to light a 100-watt bulb for four hours. It takes 95% less energy to make aluminium cans from recycled cans than to make them from raw ore.

"To reduce" balances the importance of things. Do people own possessions or do possessions own them? A spiritual question. Consumption aims at completing a person, enhancing a person, making that person whole. Frivolous consumption, conversely, dissipates the spirit. Reusing while the product still has function and utility is an example of good stewardship.

 Recycling connects people with future generations and recognises the interdependence of all life. It also reflects about personal responsibility and patterns of consumption. In this light, recycling becomes a deeply spiritual matter.

Part of global responsibility and an ethic of consumption recognises the stewardship of creation and a fairness about the use of resources. Both reusing and recycling save resources, and hence, make them more available for others.

Treasures on earth

Jesus gave a very clear command, "Do not lay up for yourselves treasures on earth, where moth and rust destroy and where thieves break in and steal[8]..." Let's look at some reasons why, and how to recognise it if we are doing so.

Why is He telling them 'don't store up for yourselves treasures on earth? Well, simply, they will not last. If you know Jesus, you are going to heaven - then every day of your lives that your treasures are in heaven you are getting closer to your treasures instead of moving away from them. If you spend your life moving away from your

---

8. Matthew 6:19

treasures, you've reason to despair. Jesus says moving towards your treasure, towards heaven gives reason to rejoice.

Imagine your life as a line, stretching from the moment you were conceived, not just physically in the womb but much earlier as a unique thought of God, to eternity. Your life on that line is a very small dot. You are living in that dot right now, but if we're smart, we'll not live for the dot but live for the line and for the people of God.

God is eternal, people will live forever, and His word will live forever. So, live your life now, while you're in the dot, in light of the line, invest in the line. That's what's going to matter after you die.

Let's look at some other reasons why Jesus tells us not to lay up treasures on earth.

Firstly, it is a poor investment. Moth and rust destroy them. The forces of nature are unstable, and decay and deterioration are built in. Inflation slowly takes away the value of our money. Identity theft and digital theft through phishing and many other types of deception can easily steal our assets. Governments tax and investments go sour.

Secondly, it affects the human spirit. Contentment and satisfaction are very fleeting. The joy at something new soon goes away, leaving us wanting the next thing. We often fear the loss of that which we are relying on, be it a bank balance, possessions, sufficient return on investments. There is often an inordinate need to preserve and protect. Thomas Watson wrote, "The soul is a spiritual thing, riches are of an earthly extract, and how can these fill a spiritual substance? How man does thirst after the world, but, alas, it falls short of his expectation. It cannot fill the hiatus and longing of his soul."

Randy Alcorn writes, "Materialism is the mother of anxiety. No wonder Christ's discourse on earthly and heavenly treasures is immediately followed by his admonitions not to worry about material things[9]. People lay up treasures on earth rather than in heaven not only because of greed and selfishness, but also because of fear and insecurity. Yet putting our hope in earthly treasures does nothing but multiply anxiety. Why? Because earthly treasures are so temporary and uncertain."

How can you discern if you are laying up treasures on earth? The first sign, according to Jesus, is that it will capture your heart. "Where your treasure is, there shall your heart be also[10]." What do you value most …? What do you think of the most? What would you most hate to lose? What are you relying on to see you through life? What do your thoughts turn to most frequently when we are free to think of what we will?

Four thousand years ago one man made a series of little choices. He was rugged, handsome, hardworking, honest, athletic, strong—and proud. Who was he? Esau, firstborn son of Isaac, grandson of God's friend Abraham, natural heir to all the promised blessings of the God of the Universe—and one who had everything that really matters in life, except the most important element. As the firstborn son of Isaac, Esau began with every imaginable opportunity and blessing; he lived with every earthly success, he died surrounded by an abundance of everything but God in his life. He sold his birthright for a small meal[11]. His treasure was right here on earth.

One of my favourite paintings is from Rembrandt, who was born in my hometown of Leiden in Holland. Unfortunately, it now hangs in Berlin, not here! Rembrandt painted a wonderful picture of The Rich Fool in 1627. Jesus taught, "The land of a rich man produced abundantly. And he thought to himself, 'What should I do, for I have no place to store my crops?'

Then he said, 'I will do this: I will pull down my barns and build larger ones, and there I will store all my grain and my

9. Matthew 6:25-34
10. Matthew 6:21
11. Genesis 25:31-34

goods. And I will say to my soul, Soul, you have ample goods laid up for many years; relax, eat, drink, be merry.' But God said to him, 'You fool! This very night your life is being demanded of you. And the things you have prepared, whose will they be[12]?'" Note how the words attributed to the rich man focus entirely on himself. He utters a soliloquy that repeatedly uses the first person singular in just three verses—" I" six times and "my" five times, in addition to speaking to his "soul." The man's deliberations demonstrate his (fatal) error. He takes no account of others, and, most importantly, takes no account of God.

He decides to build new storage facilities, not just for the bumper crop, but for all his "goods" as well. These possessions, he thinks, will ensure his well-being for "many years." That decision earns him the title "fool" from God—in the only instance of God being a (direct) character in a parable of Jesus.

The antidote for this self-entered sufficiency is given by Paul speaking to his disciple, Timothy. "As for the rich in this present age, charge them not to be arrogant, nor to set their hopes on the uncertainty of riches, but on God, who richly provides us with everything to enjoy. They are to do good, to be rich in good works, to be generous and ready to share, thus storing up treasure for themselves as a good foundation for the future, so that they may take hold of that which is truly life[13]."

Treasures in heaven

We are invited to invest in an 'eternity portfolio.' A portfolio is an overview or collection of your achievements and possessions which you have gained through life on the basis of which you are desiring meaningful rewards. A portfolio of investments will give you financial rewards; a portfolio of your experiences and works will get your desired employment. A student portfolio is a collection of your

---

12. Luke 12:16-20
13. 1 Timothy 6:17-19

work to gain a degree and a design portfolio will get you assignments. An eternity portfolio will get you rewards.

What could an 'eternity portfolio' look like? Considering the aspects of the Great Commission[14] and the Great Commandment[15], we could identify five areas of investment potential. To love God and love your neighbour. To make disciples in all nations, teaching them and baptising them. Here are five eternal funds to invest in!

1.   Treasury Fund

Investing in loving God could be a Treasury Fund - investing in the Church, Gods storehouse.

"Bring the full tithe into the storehouse, that there may be food in my house. And thereby put me to the test, says the Lord of hosts, if I will not open the windows of heaven for you and pour down for you a blessing until there is no more need. I will rebuke the devourer for you, so that it will not destroy the fruits of your soil, and your vine in the field shall not fail to bear, says the Lord of hosts[16]."

2.   Service Fund

Investing in the command to love you neighbour could be developing a Service Fund - helping the poor and needy.

"Sell your possessions, and give to the needy. Provide yourselves with moneybags that do not grow old, with a treasure in the heavens that does not fail, where no thief approaches and no moth destroys. For where your treasure is, there will your heart be also[17]."

3.   Global Fund

Investing in the commission to 'go and make disciples in all nations' could be your Global Fund, supporting missions and evangelism.

---

14. Matthew 28:18-20
15. Matthew 22:34-40
16. Malachi 3:10,1
17. Luke 12:33,34

"The master commended the dishonest manager for his shrewdness. For the sons of this world are more shrewd in dealing with their own generation than the sons of light. And I tell you, make friends for yourselves by means of unrighteous wealth, so that when it fails they may receive you into the eternal dwellings[18]."

4. Growth Fund

Investing in the command to teach people to obey all Jesus commands could be your Growth Fund, investing in teaching opportunities.

"Do not lay up for yourselves treasures on earth, where moth and rust destroy and where thieves break in and steal, but lay up for yourselves treasures in heaven, where neither moth nor rust destroys and where thieves do not break in and steal. For where your treasure is, there your heart will be also. "The eye is the lamp of the body. So, if your eye is healthy, your whole body will be full of light, but if your eye is bad, your whole body will be full of darkness. If then the light in you is darkness, how great is the darkness[19]!"

5. Mutual Fund

Investing in the command to baptise people into the life of the Trinity, to be part of the fellowship in the Body could be your Mutual Fund.

"They are to do good, to be rich in good works, to be generous and ready to share, thus storing up treasure for themselves as a good foundation for the future, so that they may take hold of that which is truly life[20]."

When money and possessions are spent on heavenly treasure, the equation changes radically. The investment takes on eternal value. Since God, his Word, and people are eternal, what will last is what is used wisely for God, his Word, and his people.

---

18. Luke 16:9,10
19. Matthew 6:19-22
20. 1 Timothy 6:17

Rewards

God grants rewards for many things, including doing good works[21], denying ourselves[22], showing compassion to the needy[23], and treating our enemies kindly[24]. He also grants us rewards for sacrificial and generous giving: "Go, sell your possessions and give to the poor, and you will have treasure in heaven[25]."

What should we think of when considering eternal rewards?

I believe the most important thing is enjoying a perfect relationship with Jesus in heaven. It is said that all life is a treasure hunt for a perfect person in a perfect place! What better reward to receive than to hear from Jesus, "Well done, good and faithful servant, enter into the joy of your master!"

In several places, the Bible also mentions a position of authority, reigning with Jesus Himself. Some will be put "in charge of many things[26]." Christ spoke of granting some followers rulership over cities—in proportion to their faithful service in managing his assets[27]. Endurance to the end is a necessary qualification. "To him who overcomes and does my will to the end, I will give authority over the nations... just as I have received authority from my Father. I will also give him the morning star[28]."

The list is almost too long to detail and out of the scope of this book, but here are some indications of what awaits the faithful. The Bible also names 'crowns' as rewards. The crown of life for being faithful in losing your life for His sake; an incorruptible crown for

---

21. Ephesians 6:8; Romans 2:6, 10
22. Matthew 16:24-27
23. Luke 14:13-14
24. Luke 6:35
25. Matthew 19:21
26. Matthew 25:21-23
27. Luke 19:17-24)
28. Revelation 2:26-28

victory in your Christian life; a crown of joy over the people you have influenced with the gospel; a crown of glory for faithfully carrying out leadership tasks, and a crown of righteousness given for getting ready for Christ's return in holy and pure living. The greatest joy will be to be able to lay all these crowns at Jesus' feet, giving Him the glory and honour!

We are promised other rewards, such as 'hidden manna,' 'a white stone,' and 'a pillar in God's temple.'

We will be allowed to eat from the tree of life in Paradise, receive praise from the angels and given new, white robes, a new name and a new home in a new city where justice and love reign – shalom and provision for all!

C.S. Lewis quoted "Indeed, if we consider the unblushing promises of reward and the staggering nature of the rewards promised in the Gospels, it would seem that Our Lord finds our desires, not too strong, but too weak. We are half-hearted creatures, fooling about with drink and sex and ambition when infinite joy is offered us, like an ignorant child who wants to go on making mud pies in a slum because he cannot imagine what is meant by the offer of a holiday at the sea. We are far too easily pleased."

Investing in People

I consider the ultimate investment to be 'investing in people.' Jesus said,' "And I tell you, make friends for yourselves by means of unrighteous wealth, so that when it fails they may receive you into the eternal dwellings[29]."

I am so moved by the film "Schindler's List" which also portrays economic persecution of Jews by a German industrialist during the War. The film begins with the alcoholic and womanizer Oskar Schindler boasting about how much money he is going to make in his factory, using free Jewish slave labour. The irony is that the

---

29. Luke 16:9

factory in Krakow was started by Jewish capital investment and the chief accountant was a Jew Itzhak Stern, who later became Schindler's conscience and helped to save many Jewish workers from extermination. Schindler made a list of Jews which were "essential" to the production efforts. In the wake of the advancing red Army, Schindler had to leave. He packs a car in the night and bids farewell to his workers. They give him a letter explaining he is not a criminal to them, together with a ring secretly made from a worker's gold dental bridge and engraved with a Talmudic quotation, "Whoever saves one life saves the world entire." Schindler is touched but deeply ashamed, feeling he could have done more to save many more lives … this is the conversation with Stern as he says his farewell to the Jews.

> **Schindler:** I could've got more... I could've got more, if I'd just...I could've got more...
> **Stern:** Oscar, there are eleven hundred people who are alive because of you. Look at them.
> **Schindler:** If I'd made more money...I threw away so much money, you have no idea. If Id just...
> **Stern:** There will be generations because of what you did.
> **Schindler:** I didn't do enough.
> **Stern:** You did so much.
> **Schindler:** This car. Goeth (the SS commander) would've bought this car. Why did I keep the car? Ten people, right there. Ten people, ten more people...(He rips the swastika pin from his lapel) This pin, two people. This is gold. Two more people. He would've given me two for it. At least one. He would've given me one. One more. One more person. A person, Stern. For this. I could've gotten one more person and I didn't. I didn`t...

Herein lies an enormous challenge for us, as Christians, today - using the money and assets which God has given us to help save lives.

Schindler is a constant reminder of questions which God is asking me. Am I wasting money? Am I growing in generosity? Am I helping to set people free?

An eternal perspective on wealth creation

John Wesley knew grinding poverty as a child. His father, Samuel Wesley, was the Anglican priest in one of England's lowest-paying parishes.

It probably came as a surprise to John Wesley that while God had called him to follow his father's vocation, he had not also called him to be poor like his father. Instead of being a parish priest, John felt God's direction to teach at Oxford University. There he was elected a fellow of Lincoln College, and his financial status changed dramatically. His position usually paid him at least thirty pounds a year, more than enough money for a single man to live on. John seems to have enjoyed his relative prosperity. He spent his money on playing cards, tobacco, and brandy.

While at Oxford, an incident changed his perspective on money. He had just finished paying for some pictures for his room when one of the chambermaids came to his door. It was a cold winter day, and he noticed that she had nothing to protect her except a thin linen gown. He reached into his pocket to give her some money to buy a coat but found he had too little left. Immediately the thought struck him that the Lord was not pleased with the way he had spent his money. He asked himself,

"Will thy Master say, "Well done, good and faithful steward"? Thou hast adorned thy walls with the money which might have screened this poor creature from the cold! O justice! O mercy! Are not these pictures the blood of this poor maid?"

Perhaps as a result of this incident, in 1731 Wesley began to limit his expenses so that he would have more money to give to the poor. He records that one year his income was 30 pounds and his living expenses 28 pounds, so he had 2 pounds to give away. The next year his income doubled, but he still managed to live on 28 pounds, so he had 32 pounds to give to the poor. In the third year, his income jumped to 90 pounds. Instead of letting his expenses rise with his income, he kept them to 28 pounds and gave away 62 pounds. In the fourth year, he received 120 pounds. As before, his expenses were 28 pounds, so his giving rose to 92 pounds.

Wesley felt that the Christian should not merely tithe but give away all extra income once the family and creditors were taken care of. He believed that with increasing income, what should rise is not the Christian's standard of living but the standard of giving.

His lifestyle was measured by his statement, *"I value all things by the price they shall gain in eternity."*

Martin Luther said, " There are only two days on my calendar... today and that day ..." All our financial decisions should be made in the light of eternity ... one day we will have to stand before Jesus and give an account of what we have dome with what he has entrusted us with.

Will your decisions count for eternity?

WHEN ALL ELSE FAILS

There are about 14 famines described in the Bible. Space does not allow me to describe all of these economic disasters, which caused severe problems for the people. Let me just describe a few, from which we can learn some lessons. Famine is like a recession or depression and causes great suffering. What does God want to teach his people through these hard times?

Famine throughout the Middle East

Genesis 47 tells of probably the most widespread recorded famine.

Joseph had a dream and foretold 7 very bad years. We read that their money was all gone[1]. Clearly, people were not prepared for hard times. Then we read that they had to sell their livestock in exchange to buy grain for bread[2]. They were forced to sell valuable assets, probably for severely discounted prices.

Then, the situation got so bad, that they were forced to sell their land for food, thereby destroying their future[3].

Finally, they were so desperate after selling all their livestock and land, they got to the point of realisation that all they had left were

1. Genesis 47:15
2. Genesis 47:16
3. Genesis 47:19

their bodies. They asked Pharaoh to take them into slavery[4].

Joseph taxed the grain which was given to the people at 20% but the people lost their land and became slaves to the system.

Bad times will come. We must learn to save for the future. Joseph's example of saving 20% turned out to be the very way in which the people could survive. He had sufficient seed to be able to distribute. Joseph was a good steward.

Fleeing from Famine

Ruth 1:1 tells us a famine caused a husband and wife to leave Bethlehem and go to Moab. The move to Moab seems to help the family and Elimelech, Naomi, Mahlon, Kilion, Orpha, and they were quite happy in Moab. However, disaster struck again some years later. First Elimelech died and then his two sons, leaving the women in a desperate situation. In the society of that time, death of supporting male family members greatly impacted the women, economically. The situation seemed hopeless and they concluded, "the hand of the Lord has gone out against us[5]." They suffered again from lack of food.

Naomi leaves Moab hoping to find food in Bethlehem where she had heard that the famine was over. The town was excited at seeing them again, but Naomi said, "Call me Mara, because the Almighty has made life very bitter for me[6]. Why call me Naomi when the Lord has caused me to suffer and the Almighty has sent such tragedy upon me?" She went on to say, "God has brought me home." She sees all of these unfortunate events of famine and death as somehow a work of the Lord.

The story has a happy ending. Daughter Ruth meets Boaz and they get married. They have a son and name him Obed. Obed is the

---

4. Genesis 47:19
5. Ruth 1:13
6. Ruth 1:21

father of Jessie who is the father of David, and these are mentioned in the genealogy of Jesus Christ[7].

We see that God was using these economic conditions to physically move people to the locations they needed to be and to meet people they needed to meet.

God uses economic difficulties to prepare people for His glory. Those situations are painful, but, in all things we see that God uses the waste products of life to make something beautiful! God is in the re-cycling business!

Drought in Samaria

The third famine is described in 1 Kings 18. It lasted three and a half years, and the people suffered great under the wicked leaders, Ahab and Jezebel. When rain stops in that part of the world, the economy stops. God had a   faithful steward in Obadiah, who was able to feed a hundred of Gods prophets. Impressed, Ahab told Obadiah to go and look elsewhere for grass to feed the horses and mules, because the livestock was about to die. This became so critical that Ahab did not want to lose his assets.

Obadiah found Elisha. Elisha went to Ahab and told him that the famine would not end because Ahab was following the prophets of Baal. The struggle culminated in Mount Carmel at the big test between Elisha and the prophets of Baal.

Fire came when Elisha called out to God, and Elisha was able to tell Ahab that the rains would come. God used this economic pain to turn the hearts of the people back to God - and they acknowledged God to be in control of rain, fire and economy - not the powerful Ahab, Jezebel or Baal.

---

7. Matthew 1:5

A terrible famine

We can read this awful famine, together with a war in 2 Kings 6 to 8. Terrible times in a combination of disasters.

The king of Syria gathered his army and besieged Samaria and people starved[8]. This siege lasted so long, that famine ensued. People were so desperate for food that they were buying a donkeys head at an enormous price of 80 shekels of silver, almost a kilogram, equivalent today to about $650. They were buying a quarter of a seed pod for five shekels of silver. Birds passed these seed pods after they ate them[9]. Talk about hyperinflation!

This famine became so bad that they started to eat one another. We read of a woman who cried out for help, because others wanted to kill and eat her babies. [10] In this time of war, people could not even surrender because they would be killed. The besieged king was at his wit's end and was desperate to get out of the mess. He could not solve the problem.

He needed to look to God, who was using economic pain to help them realise that God controls the economy. Elisha passed on God's promise. "At this time tomorrow, at the gates of the city, about 20 kilos of fine flour will sell for a shekel - about $ 10 in today's money. God told them the exact time, the exact commodity, at the exact place. No-one knew what the price of commodities would be … but the man of God did.

A senior officer stood next to the king. He said, "If the Lord himself should make windows in heaven, how could this thing be?" He could just not believe that God could do something like that! They were in the middle of war and hyper-inflation! Elisha looked at him and replied, "You shall see it with your own eyes, but you shall not

---

8. 2 Kings 6:24
9. 2 Kings 6:25
10. 2 Kings 6:29

eat of it[11]." Elisha was bold confident because he knew God.   He ended self-reliance. It is not up to us!

Everything came out as predicted and actually happened the next day by a miracle of God[12]. The captain was trampled at the gate. Who do we trust rational man or the man of God?

Universal famine in the 1st century AD

The early, emerging church was confronted with a widespread famine. During the reign of Claudius Caesar, several different famines are known to have occurred. In the fourth year of his office, 45 A.D., a famine was particularly severe in Judea and described by Luke[13], and lasted about three years.   Josephus, the Jewish historian, supplied further information concerning the intensity of this famine, with its great distress and many deaths.

The famine served as an occasion for many of the New Testament congregations to co-operate in the giving of material aid to the fellow believers who lived in Judea.

Just before this famine, prophets had journeyed from Jerusalem to Antioch, and one by the name of Agabus, inspired by the Holy Spirit, proclaimed that there would be "great lack throughout all the world," and then Luke says, "this came to pass in the days of Claudius Caesar."

The next verse informs us that the disciples in Antioch, were determined to send relief to the believers in Judea. Each man, according to his ability would make a donation, which, in turn, was sent to the "elders by the hands of Barnabas and Saul[14]."

The disciples started to care for one another. Suffering produced

---

11. 2 Kings 7:2
12. 2 Kings 7:16
13. Acts 11:28
14. Acts 11:30

unity. Suffering divides the world but can unify the Body of Christ through their support. In economic disasters, the world will be full of fear and people will panic. We will deliver hope. The famine was, in fact, perfectly timed to bring the Church together, to invest in each other, and to see how God delivers His solutions through His people.

Throughout the famines, God wanted people to learn lessons and trust in Him for the outcome. When facing troubling economic times, take heart! His promises remain true and solid. "Behold, the eye of the Lord is on those who fear him, on those who hope in his steadfast love, that he may deliver their soul from death and keep them alive in famine[15]."

"The Lord knows the days of the blameless, and their heritage will remain forever; they are not put to shame in evil times; in the days of famine they have abundance[16]."

Economic collapse foretold by James

The apostle James wrote, "Come now, you rich, weep and howl for the miseries that are coming upon you. Your riches have rotted and your garments are moth-eaten. Your gold and silver have corroded, and their corrosion will be evidence against you and will eat your flesh like fire. You have laid up treasure in the last days[17]."

This verse predicts that, "In the last days" the rich will "heap up treasures" by exploiting the poor, but that the Lord will take note and their treasures will be "a witness against" them. The treasures on which they have built their security will fail.

James wrote this in Jerusalem around AD 47, perhaps the first writing of an apostle. It was a time of spiritual insecurity. Questions were being raised such as, 'Do you have to keep the Jewish laws and be circumcised in order to be saved?' It was also a time of political and

---

15. Psalm 33:18,19
16. Psalm 37:19
17. James 5:1-3

military oppression by the Romans and a time of oppression by the rich Jewish elite.   Jerusalem was the centre of the Temple's banking system, run by the Pharisees, who, according to Luke, were 'lazy and 'turned up their noses' in front of Jesus.' The Temple dominated the country's economy.

The Pharisees led a bank, in which money, earned from sacrifices was kept... together with Temple taxes, currency gains, and other commercial activities. Swiss theologians Eckhard and Wolfgang Stegemann compared the first-century Jerusalem with modern Switzerland. "The Jerusalem Temple had become the safest bank in the Middle East because of its many privileges. In terms of investment, it enjoyed the respect that Switzerland enjoys today. Many foreigners, merchants and politicians kept accounts there - a lucrative business for the Temple Bank, because of the deposit taxes it levied".

You can get an idea of the extent of this banking operation, reading about Crassus, an advisor to Caesar, who 'plundered the Temple treasury and went away with 8,000 talents gold and 2,000 talents silver'... equivalent of 6 billion euros today!

Their wealth would not last long... the Temple was completely destroyed in AD 70... 50 tons of gold and silver transported under Vespasian and his son Titus and brought to Rome, which paid for the Colosseum. They would really experience the prophecy of James in verse 2 here! "Your riches have perished! James starts his prophecy with... 'Now then...'. Come on... listen!

That on which the economy of Jerusalem was built, collapsed. The economic problems caused the Church to scatter and grow.

To whom is this prophecy addressed? When you want to talk about poverty and wealth, you have to deal with 4 groups of people.

> There are some who are poor on the outside and poor on the inside. They do not have any of the goods of the world and at the same time know nothing about Jesus Christ or God's love. They are the ones who need to be helped spiritually and in a material sense.

Then there are people who are poor on the outside and rich on the inside. They have few possessions but are born again and have eternal life. They are generous and confident.

Some are rich on the outside and also rich on the inside. They have many material goods and they also have a close relationship with God. We know people in the world who are like that and in the Bible there were many, like Abraham, Joseph, Daniel, Job, Joseph of Arimathea, and so on. They are good stewards and generous!

Then there are those who are rich on the outside and poor on the inside. They have much wealth but have no foundation of Jesus in their lives. This is the group to which James writes. In his time there was an elite who had the lives of most people in their hands.

The people in the second and third groups will be able to flourish in any economic times. When the system fails, not technical solution will save us - only faith and trust in the Lord's goodness.

The Fall of Rome

Christians of all eras can have their faith strengthened and their wariness of the seductive world system heightened by Revelation 18.

I want to highlight how one of the most important theologians in the history of the church dealt with the reality of the fall of Babylon in his own time. His name is Augustine of Hippo.

When the Visigoths ransacked Rome in 410 AD, the reaction throughout the empire was very similar to the shock throughout the United States after 9/11. Many Christians were sure that this event was sign of the soon return of Christ. The fact that Christian churches were spared the brunt of destruction further spread an apocalyptic view.

The separation of the empire between Constantinople (in Asia Minor) and Rome brought about the very decline in trade that is foretold in Revelation 18. People were asking difficult questions:

- How could this happen?

- Is God not on our side?

- Aren't we a Christian nation?

- Is this the judgment of God?

- Does Rome have a future?

Is this what was prophesied in Revelation 18 (the majority view of church history has been to equate Babylon with Rome)?

O these questions sound familiar? We are asking them today, too.

In his magnum opus, The City of God, Augustine is not able to adequately answer all of the questions surrounding the calamities of the decline of Rome. He does, however, give Christians a theology of history that allows us to see and contrast the City of God (Jerusalem) with the City of Man (Babylon) throughout every age of Biblical and post-Biblical history.

In our own day, we should be able to identify many of the goods of Babylon that cannot satisfy and will not last. These are all summed up in power, privilege, pleasure, and value. He challenges the reader to set their sights higher than a mere earthly empire.

The fall of Babylon certainly involves economic collapse. Plagues destroy any sense of the pleasure and satisfaction that people sought to buy from the wares of the city. Trade comes to a halt. Incomes vanish. Jobs go away.

Verse 19 tells us that in one hour the rich city has been laid waste. Many of us received a taste of what this feels like in 2008. Jobs, investments, homes, cars, and all of the nice things that money can buy disappeared in a matter of months. Times like this can cause great anguish and depression — especially for people who worship the power, privilege, pleasure, and value of Babylon.

The message for the church is clear: Babylon is an incredibly seductive place. We must be constantly watchful if we are going to remain separate from this worldly ethos and focused on the worship of God.

I can give example after example of born-again Christians who have seen their lives shipwrecked by consumerism, debt, sexual immorality, worshipping of titles, positions, jobs, sports, education, and love for the raw power of leadership positions.

The book, the 'City of God' was motivated by the sack of Rome in A.D. 410 by the Visigoths in a dispute over payment for Visigoth mercenaries. Though they were not pagans, the Visigoths were not Christian either – they were Arian heretics. The city of Rome had long since lost its political and economic significance for the Empire, but it still held a great symbolic and psychological importance; Rome was 'the Eternal City', 'Coeval with the universe and secure while the laws of nature held.' Its destruction sent shockwaves rippling throughout the Empire, and as often happens in times of crisis, people looked for someone to blame. The pagans fixed upon the Christians as their target; Rome had fallen, so they argued, because the worship of the old gods had been abandoned and the pagan religion had been disestablished. The gods had, they said, retaliated by withdrawing their protection from those who no longer worshipped them. Many Christians reacted with stunned despair, reasoning that if Rome had fallen, the end of the world was at hand.

Augustine's reaction was different, the calm response of faith. He set to answering the objections of the pagans and calming the fears of the Christians. Instead of panicking, the Christian philosopher's mind was stimulated to investigate the very nature of history itself. He cut Rome down to size; far from being the ideal, the final state, it was another empire like any other, and as earlier empires had fallen, so too Rome itself might pass away; it was neither unique nor irreplaceable. Others idealised Rome; he called for a healthy realism where all human institutions were concerned.

History was, Augustine explained, 'a tale of two cities', the City of God and the Earthly City, which 'Two states are intimately connected and promiscuously blended with one another in this life until they are separated by the final judgement.'

Cain and Abel were the archetypes of the two cities, Cain the founder of the earthly city, Abel a citizen of the Eternal. These two states have been created by two different sets of affections, the earthly by the love of self to the contempt of God; the heavenly by the love of God to the contempt of self. That one glories in self; this one in God.' The City of God is a stranger in the world, it is not Rome, and it is to be identified with no human city, state or system; its founder is God himself.

In his book, 'A Tale of Two Cities,' Charles Dickens described the paradox we are in today.

"It was the best of times, it was the worst of times, it was the age of wisdom, it was the age of foolishness, it was the epoch of belief, it was the epoch of incredulity, it was the season of light, it was the season of darkness, it was the spring of hope, it was the winter of despair."

These conflicts between wisdom and foolishness, belief and unbelief, light and darkness, hope and despair will continue. Learning to live and working in God's economy will bring us wisdom, belief, light and hope.

Destruction of the world economic system.

I believe that mammon, the fallen power behind money which Jesus unmasked[18], will get such a grip on our economy, that eventually, people will not be able to buy or sell, unless they obey mammon's system.

After warning about the false teachings of the world's political and

---

18. Luke 6:13

religious systems and their rebellion against God, Revelation speaks of economic persecution against those who refuse to go along with the prevailing religious and political powers: "He also forced everyone, small and great, rich and poor, free and slave, to receive a mark on his right hand or on his forehead, so that no one could buy or sell unless he had the mark, which is the name of the beast or the number of his name[19]."

A final and complete collapse is ahead of us, and it is described for us in Revelation 18. I think we are all curious about the current state of the world economically and in particular the one-world economy we have today. Up until really recent years there was an economy in this country and that country and very little really coming together. That isn't true anymore. We are living in a time of global commerce and a one-world economy.

And that all fits into the final picture prophetically in the book of Revelation. We are interested in what's coming down the road because we're planning our future financially. We're interested in stock markets and interest rates and budget deficits. Our interest is fuelled because it fills the newspapers, the magazines and is on the radio and television, where they discuss all things political and economic. More than ever in the history of the world are we living in a one-world economy and our own future is tied to what's going on globally. We are not isolated anymore. Our economy affects the entire globe and therefore our investments and our economics, our money and our future are really controlled by events, circumstances and people and nations over which we have very little or no control.

What about the future? Will this world economy continue? Will it even become stronger? The answer is yes. And the book of Revelation tells us that that will happen. There will be increasing materialism. Capitalism will prevail.

As the book of Revelation unfolds, the judgments of God will be poured out, prior to the day of the Lord; there is going to be chaos in

---

19. Revelation 13:16, 17

the world, but amazingly the world will survive with some measure of economic prosperity.

This theme is expanded in Revelation 18, describing the fall of Babylon, which pictures the whole world getting rich off the global trade that Babylon generates. We see, in Revelation 18, the final world economy described under the name Babylon. You'll notice in verse 2, "Fallen, fallen is Babylon the great."

This is the final world economic system. This will happen prior to the Second Coming of Jesus Christ. It describes the world flourishing economically just before the Lord Jesus comes in final judgment. So, a worldwide economic boom will come. It will consume the whole world, a one world global economy built on lust for luxury, materialism. Capitalism will reach its apex under Satan and the Antichrist. It will be hammered by judgment from God, but it will survive until finally God pronounces its doom.

Economic disasters ahead

Revelation 18 lists in detail the luxury items that Babylon had been purchasing, and how "the merchants of the earth have become rich through the abundance of her luxury."[20] However, she will be judged and her wealth destroyed: "In the measure that she glorified herself and lived luxuriously, in the same measure give her torment and sorrow… she will be utterly burned with fire" (vs. 7,8).

Her ruin will bring global trade to an end: "And the merchants of the earth… who became rich by her… will weep and mourn over her, for no one buys their merchandise anymore… Alas, alas, that great city, in which all who had ships on the sea became rich by her wealth! For in one hour she is made desolate" (vs. 11, 15, 19).

Revelation 11 implies that during the time when the Two Witnesses will be giving the last message to the world, there will be a severe drought, which usually results in a more general financial crisis.

---

20. Revelation 18:3

"These (the Two Witnesses) have power to shut heaven, so that no rain falls in the days of their prophecy[21]." The prophet Joel also predicts this drought. "The Day of the Lord is at hand... the seed shrivels under the clods, storehouses are in shambles; barns are broken down for the grain has withered... The beasts of the field also cry out to (the Lord), for the water brooks are dried up[22]."

The great financial crisis ahead will be only one aspect of a more general crisis which is called "the Great Tribulation[23]," "The Time of Trouble such as never was[24]," "The Day of the Lord[25]," and "the Hour of Trial which shall come upon the whole world[26]."

Although the Great Tribulation will make all previous crises pale in comparison, God will preserve those who love Him during that time— "He who walks righteously and speaks uprightly, who despises the gain of oppressions, who shakes his hands, lest they hold a bribe, who stops his ears from hearing of bloodshed and shuts his eyes from looking on evil, he will dwell on the heights; his place of defence will be the fortresses of rocks; his bread will be given him; his water will be sure[27]."

"Though the fig tree may not blossom, nor fruit be on the vines; Though the labour of the olive may fail, and the fields yield no food; Though the flock may be cut off from the fold, and there be no herd in the stalls— Yet I will rejoice in the Lord, I will joy in the God of my salvation[28]."

---

21. Revelation 11:6
22. Joel 1:15-20
23. Matthew 24:21
24. Daniel 12:1
25. Joel 1:15
26. Revelation 3:10
27. Isaiah 33:15,16
28. Habakkuk 3:17,18

Personal crises

I would like to share with you two crises in my business life during which I learned a lot. The lessons learned from these crises have helped me through many subsequent crises.

The first was when I was 30 years old, director of a chemical company. We were enjoying success in business, but I discovered I was being a failure in life. My success came at a high price in three packages; firstly, my health, then my marriage and lastly, my faith. The cost was too high. I was climbing the ladder of success, and when I reached the top, I discovered that my ladder was leaning against the wrong wall. I saw openly disillusionment around me. Poor health, a failing marriage and a faith in God which had no practical relevance to my business and private life.

However, years before, in the sixties, I had had an encounter with Jesus of Nazareth which I never forgot. This was a time of free love, experimenting with drugs, rebelling against all authority and a search for meaning in life. Jesus showed me that He, amongst many other gods on offer at the time, was the way, the truth and the life. As a student I embraced Jesus and started to follow him. He became the centre of my life. But I had never learned to apply this faith to my business life. They were two different realms.

During this first crisis, I discovered again the foundation of my faith; that there was a God who loved me and wanted me, and who sent Jesus to show me the way to a life of fellowship with God. Jesus would not let me go. He was there in my life, speaking to me. I got help from my wife and some fellow Christians in business to re-order my priorities. I discovered again the Bible which has so much to say about life and work.

The second crisis was just a few months after I had taken over as CEO of a space services business. First of all we survived a scare when during a launch in Baikonur, Kazakhstan, a Proton rocket came crashing down and almost killed one of our employees.

Then, in February 2002, the space shuttle crashed on its way home to Cape Kennedy over the Texas plains. We had experiments on board, and we knew the commander, Rick Husband. He was a Christian and had left a series of messages for his family 'just in case' he never returned. He didn't.

In one of these messages he said, " If anything should happen, don't worry. I will be going even higher!" His funeral was a celebration of his life. Family and friends were thankful for him and his testimony to the faithfulness of God. Jesus was at the centre of his life and his family had a strong core of faith which saw them through the crisis.

On the Sunday before the men went into quarantine for their space flight, the congregation at Grace Community Church prayed for the astronauts. Said fellow astronaut Mike Anderson at the time: "Rick and I have prayed for a successful mission, but also that somehow God would allow everyone to see our faith in Him." His prayer was answered.

During this crisis, I realised that no crisis, even a catastrophe of such proportions, will ever separate us from God's love for us, and His promise of eternal life.

Solutions

So, how can we weather the storms of crisis? How can we organise ourselves so that we can weather future storms?

It has been said, that the four top characteristics of our economy today are Greed, Pride, Power and Fear. The economics of the Kingdom will help us to overcome these four storms of the economy of the world which come over us. Overcome greed with generosity and sharing. Overcome pride and show humility. Use power in serving others. Dismantle fear and experience peace.

One of America's most influential Christian financial planners, Ron Blue, told of how he was summoned before a congressional committee to give advice on combatting economic problems. He gave the chairman who was a US Senator a solution to remaining strong in a crisis. He proposed six disciplines which will see you through in any economic situation. Ron Blue, when giving these 6 points was almost apologetic for their simplicity.

- Work as a steward - not an owner. We should be good managers, responsible, transparent and accountable with the use of other people's resources!

- Spend less than you earn over a long period of time; the answer to economic success!

- Steer clear from debt, because debt mortgages the future and removes freedom.

- Build reserves, liquidity to help you survive in difficult times and save for future wants.

- Learn to be generous because this shares the wealth and breaks the power of mammon.

- Set long term goals to build wealth for ourselves, our children, church and business.

The senator replied, "If only our nation could embrace these simple truths... we would all be much better off!"

And personally?

Gandhi said, "Be the change that you wish to see in the world. As human beings, our greatness lies not so much in being able to remake the world – that is the myth of the atomic age – as in being able to remake ourselves." So, how can we remake ourselves?

The apostle Paul writing to Roman Christians, said, " Do not be conformed to the pattern of this world, but be transformed by the renewal of you mind, so that you may know what God was - the good, acceptable and perfect[29]!" But how can we be transformed?

---

29. Romans 12:2

That is what Jesus of Nazareth came to do.

Firstly, He gives us a fixed core – a rock which does not change in the centre of our life - in the midst of rough seas and trouble times. He has promised to give us the Spirit of God who will enable us to do what we cannot do ourselves. You cannot pull yourself up with your own shoelaces! You need a force outside yourself which gives you the necessary help to deal with the changes occurring all around us. One of the key success factors in business today is the ability to deal meaningfully with change and to adapt to the changing circumstances.

Secondly, He helps us develop loving relationships from which we receive the necessary support, advice and encouragement.

Thirdly, we do not know what the future may bring. Economic prosperity again? Disaster? Jesus will help us develop a healthy economic foundation, so that we can be content and find joy in any economic condition. The apostle Paul experienced the miracle, the secret of contentment, blessed peace in any circumstance, whether in abundance or need[30].

"Not that I am speaking of being in need, for I have learned in whatever situation I am to be content. I know how to be brought low, and I know how to abound. In any and every circumstance, I have learned the secret of facing plenty and hunger, abundance and need. I can do all things through him who strengthens me."

Fourthly, as Christians, we believe God owns everything and that He has made me a manager of His resources. This means that I do not own anything - and if I don't own anything, I cannot lose anything! He has the authority to give and to take, as old Job remarked when enduring his terrible crisis, "Naked I came from my mother's womb, and naked shall I return. The Lord gave, and the Lord has taken away; blessed be the name of the Lord[31]."

---

30. Philippians 4:11-13
31. Job 1:21

In the final analysis, only faith in the Lord remains.

GOING FORWARD

So, in the light of impending troubles, what are some key factors which will help us to ride the storm?

Surrender

The world's system will ultimately take everyone out, unless we are surrendered to the Lord. There is a huge difference between commitment and surrender. We are all one circumstance away from the inability to keep our commitments. We need to fully surrender our plans, hope, dreams and all we have to the Lord, praying, "not my will but Yours be done, o Lord." Jesus went to the cross, not by commitment but by surrender.

Renunciation is a basic requirement to flourish in the Kingdom of heaven. Jesus said to all who wanted to follow Him, "Let him deny himself and take up his cross daily and follow me. For whoever would save his life will lose it, but whoever loses his life for my sake will save it. For what does it profit a man if he gains the whole world and loses or forfeits himself[1]?" He also warned us that, "Any one of you who does not renounce all that he has cannot be my disciple[2]."

Renunciation means completely surrendering ourselves to the Lord.

---

1. Luke 9:23-25
2. Luke 14:33

It is very different from 'commitment.' Commitment means that I promise to do something for you. Surrender means I give myself completely to you.

Surrender is not easy. Hiroo Onoda, a Japanese soldier on the island of Lubang, in the Philippines, was isolated from his platoon and the rest of the world during World War 2. Despite the countless efforts to inform him that the war was over, Onoda continued the fight for 29 years until finally, on March 10, 1974 he surrendered his rusty sword to the Philippine authorities, thus becoming the last Japanese soldier to surrender. Surrendering is not easy. For those who have invited Jesus into our lives, the war is over, Jesus has gained complete victory, however surrendering is so difficult.

The process of renunciation is not without reward - not only now, but also in coming times. "And he said to them, "Truly, I say to you, there is no one who has left house or wife or brothers or parents or children, for the sake of the kingdom of God, who will not receive many times more in this time, and in the age to come eternal life[3]."

Lordship, Stewardship & Generosity

The three key success factors in learning to live and grow in God's economy are Lordship, Stewardship and Generosity.

Unfortunately, not all believers have realised the necessity to acknowledge Jesus as Lord of their lives; to surrender to His will in all their daily affairs. Lordship means finding out what the Master wants us to do and then to carry out His wishes. There is very little talk in Church about a Biblical way to manage our money, work and possessions. Talking about money in Church is even a taboo, it has become a very private area off our lives outside of the influence of the Church's teaching. We have to reclaim this area for the Lord! "Not everyone who says to me, 'Lord, Lord,' will enter the kingdom of heaven, but the one who does the will of my Father who is in

---

3. Luke 18:29

heaven[4]."

When we understand the Lordship of Christ, that He has the right to give us instructions, then we have to take the role as steward or manager of His resources. We need to realise that all we possess has been entrusted to us by the Master, who is the Owner and Sustainer and Giver of all things. Everything belongs to God and He gives us the wonderful privilege to manage money, possessions, relationships, gifts and talents on His behalf. "For it will be like a man going on a journey, who called his servants and entrusted to them his property[5]."

The ultimate proof that I am learning to obey Jesus as Lord, that I have accepted my role as manager of Gods resources, is growth in generosity. Growth in giving my time, talents and treasure for His purposes is the 'acid test' of Lordship and stewardship. "But who am I, and what is my people, that we should be able thus to offer willingly? For all things come from you, and of your own have we given you[6]."

Jubilee

Israel was supposed to turn economics from a short-term dog-eat-dog world we inhabit into a 50-year game with a reset button. The Year of Jubilee was the 'Reboot' in the system, the 'Ctrl-Alt-Del' in the universe. Jesus proclaimed Jubilee – and said, 'I am He,' the fulfilment of Jubilee. But He doesn't seem to simply have been inaugurating a Jubilee year - rather He was announcing a Jubilee age - the kingdom of God and its economy.

Essentially, there are three elements of Jubilee: Release, Return and Renewal.

---

4. Matthew 7:21
5. Matthew 24:14
6. 1 Chronicles 29:14

Release

Liberty was proclaimed to all inhabitants of the land. Slaves were freed. Today, liberation implies that we as Christians need to be the bearer of the Good News of Release to all. The world does not know it is enslaved, but we preach the news of release in Jesus Christ. Real freedom is being released from the bondage of sin to freedom in Christ. The most common slavery today is debt from which we have to work to liberate people from the yoke of over-indebtedness.

Return

Under Jubilee, land was restored to the original owners. In our context, what are we required to return to the Lord? We can return our lives to our Creator and God, for we are HIS possessions. He is our original owner! This includes our careers, families, assets and all that we have. Our lives are not our own. We are only stewards of the blessings God has given us in our task to care for his Kingdom.

Renewal

In Jubilee, the land was left idle for a year in order to rest and be renewed. The people only ate what grew naturally. What are the biblical analogies for today? Our faith is like the land or ground on which seed is scattered. In Jubilee, we can allow our faith to "grow wild" for a year by releasing ourselves from the comforts of life that we obtain through our own strengths and efforts. We can instead place our full reliance on God. This releases us from the pursuit of material wealth, to seek the Kingdom of God and his righteousness (Matthew 6:33-34). By doing this, we also find rest. Jesus said, "Come to me and I will give you rest". Are you taking time to rest in the arms of Jesus to let him renew your spirit?

Despite the language of release, rest and renewal, Jubilee is not passive but is about moving forward in faith. It is more than just accepting Christ as King and Saviour but about making him King in every area of life. It is about taking radical steps to give our all to him in full dependence and trust.

Indeed, living out the year of Jubilee is full of risks! It is about moving forward by taking risks in our lives in order to know the great grace of God.

A new capitalism

Churchill said, ""Capitalism is the worst economic system, except for all the others. The inherent vice of capitalism is the unequal sharing of blessings; the inherent virtue of socialism is the equal sharing of miseries." Although the Bible dopes not explicitly promote or defend the capitalist system, it is the best we have … but it needs to be strongly influenced by Gods economy.

I was privileged to be with Bruno Roche, Chief Economist at Mars Inc. at a meeting of the European Economic Summit, who proposed an economics of mutuality. This is based on the value of the individual.

Starting with the value of the individual, the first task is to develop and invest in Human Capital. In that way each individual relates to and interacts with others - developing Social Capital with shared identity and values. And then this should be developed within the framework of our Natural Capital, investing in environmental capital. Lastly, this all leads to developing financial capital.

Bruno Roche stated that if we start with developing Financial Capital as the primary goal, then this will always transpire to the cost of human capital, social capital and environmental capital. Financial Capital is the fruit of investing in human, social and natural capital and is needed for liquidity in the system. Financial Capital only came as a means of facilitating the exchange of goods and services allowing the economy to grow. The purpose of money is not to accumulate but to facilitate!

Focus on developing human, social and natural capital and the shared financial capital will follow. Don't follow money, money will follow you. Let us use our Financial Capital (Shekels) to set people free, enabling them to enjoy Human, Social and Natural Capital in all they do!

That is economics of mutuality ... mutual remuneration ... so that each individual involved in the economic process experiences Shalom ... peace, contentment, completeness, wholeness, well-being and harmony!

What should we do?

We also need to ask: What is our true currency, ultimately? It shouldn't be money, but faith and obedience. If we are faithful to God and follow His ways, He will give us the power to be content and thankful in any economic circumstance. In a period of widespread famine, which we discussed earlier, He fed the prophet Elijah through ravens bringing him food for many days. God can intervene in many ways to provide for His obedient and faithful servants.

As Jesus said, "Look at the birds of the air: they neither sow nor reap nor gather into barns, and yet your heavenly Father feeds them. Are you not of more value than they?"

"Therefore do not be anxious, saying, 'What shall we eat?' or 'What shall we drink?' or 'What shall we wear?' For the Gentiles seek after all these things, and your heavenly Father knows that you need them all. But seek first the kingdom of God and his righteousness, and all these things will be added to you."[7]

Yes, our protection and our ultimate currency is our faith— our trust, obedience and love of the truth. Those who have made wealth into an idol will be devastated. But God will provide for the faithful, and He has promised not to abandon us.

Jesus Christ asked in Luke 18:8, "When the Son of Man comes, will He really find faith on the earth?" Will we remain faithful? Will we seek God in times like this? Let us develop a strong faith! For as has been said of earlier difficult days, "These are the times that try men's souls"—testing their spiritual character and faith in God. When such

---

7. Matthew 6:24-33

things start to happen, we should be ready[8]."

Some questions to ponder:

Here are some questions for you to think about and meditate on the tension between the economy of the world and the economy of the kingdom of God.

Here are the nine ways to influence our world economy which we have handled in the book. Can you describe other ways?

    1.   Stewardship influencing personal property

Realising that the Lord God is Creator, Owner and Operator of the entire universe, have I taken the step to transfer all assets under my control from the common kingdom to the kingdom of heaven?

This is one of the most liberating things I have ever done. It entails a one-time decision, to say, "Lord, now I own nothing. All is yours; my time, my talents and my treasure. Following that commitment is a daily surrender to the will of the Owner, to use whatever I manage for His purposes. My role now is manager of Gods resources which He entrusts to me."

    2.   Holy Spirit overcoming the power of mammon

Realising that there is a spiritual battle going on in which the god of money, mammon is competing vigorously for my allegiance, have I acknowledged the role of the Holy Spirit in empowering me to do that which I cannot do myself?

Do I live and work out of the victory over the power of money which Jesus won on the cross, which will enable me to choose Gods plans and purposes over money? Am I choosing people, helping to set them free to be all they can be, above money?

---

8. Matthew 24:32-34

3. Building assets instead of debt

Realising that I have been set free by Christ, am I guarding this freedom by not allowing myself to become enslaved by debt?

Can I trust in the Lord's provision for all that He is asking me to do?

Am I using financial capital to build up the more important forms of wealth - spiritual capital, physical capital, relational capital, productive capital?

4. Working to serve instead of working to earn money

Realising that God has gifted me with talents, skills, wisdom and know-how, am I working hard to glorify God, ensuring His reputation in the workplace is held in esteem and is a testimony to God's excellence and service?

Am I choosing work according to His calling, or am I looking for jobs which pay the most?

How am I demonstrating agape love, as an outflowing of God's love in me, in my workplace?

5. Introducing the grace of giving and receiving to influence the transactional power of buying and selling

Realising that Jesus was bought by the Pharisees and sold by Judas, can I focus on serving the interests of others and develop covenantal relationships, walking the extra mile and looking for ways to demonstrate love in the workplace?

Can I use some of the money I have 'uneconomically' by giving to those in need?

6. Answering the question, 'How Much is Enough?" and setting limits on spending

Realising that the Lord promises to supply all we need at all times can I place a limit on my spending and answer the question 'how much is enough for me with the responsibilities I have?' Can I exercise contentment so that I can develop wealth to share?

7.   Generational planning instead of short-term thinking

Realising that the promise of the Lord's blessing is both for myself and for the generations coming after me, am I building wealth for future generations?

Am I teaching and empowering my children, and those following me in the workplace, to take up their responsibilities as good stewards of their God-given assets and assignments?

8.   Utilising the Lord's abundance instead of a scarcity mentality

Realising that our Creator God is a God of abundance, can I trust Him to work through me to create new ways and products to solve problems and serve those around me?

Can I obey whatever He asks me to do, knowing that His work, done in His way will never lack the resources to carry put the task?

How am I helping to alleviate poverty?

9.   Focussing on eternal rewards instead of mere temporal gain

Realising that my ultimate destiny is to work with the Lord into eternity, am I investing wealth in a portfolio which has eternal consequences?

Where is the focus on my 'treasures', on that which I consider the most valuable in life? On death or in heaven?

How much a motivation is thinking about eternal rewards? If I know my life here is short, and eternity is long, how should this affect my decisions today?

The Flow of Life – a vision

The prophet Ezekiel painted a picture of hope to the people of Israel, when the nation was in despair. Jerusalem had been established as a city with a temple in the city where God was present.

Then immediately that earthly power waned. The nation was divided and worship corrupted. The northern kingdom fell to Assyria. The southern kingdom rallied then was overcome by Babylon. Jerusalem was taken. The temple was destroyed, and the cream of the nation exiled. For two generations, Israel's leaders questioned, "Why has the nation been so destroyed." They found an answer. They deserved everything which happened to them.

Ezekiel wanted passionately for hope to be restored in the midst of a people in exile, and a lifeless Jerusalem. He received a grand vision, a plan for the new temple, and a promise of a life-giving flow of water. All renewal flows from a fresh and powerful vision of God.

He was given a vision of a tiny trickle of water, so small, a teardrop of grace flowing from the place of prayer and sacrifice out into the desert. The flow started as a small stream but increased and had an almost unbelievable impact.

As it flowed, the water deepened. The only measurement taken is the depth of the water of life: after one thousand cubits[9], ankle deep; after another thousand knee deep; another thousand, waist deep; Another thousand and it is deep enough to swim in, a river no one could cross.

This is living water. Everything in the story points to the power of the life it holds. It comes from God, from grace alone. The effect of the water of life on the desert where nothing grows is astounding! In the length of time it takes to walk out four thousand cubits and then back, there are trees on each side of the river. These are all kinds of trees for food. This is the new Garden of Eden. This is a new creation. There is no forbidden fruit. There is a harvest not once a year but every month.

---

9. A cubit is approximately 45 cm.

Their fruit will be for food and their leaves for healing.

Next and greatest of all there is the effect of this river on the landlocked sea south of Jerusalem known all over the world as the Dead Sea.

What happens when this tiny trickle of water, this teardrop from the place of prayer and sacrifice, has grown into a stream and then a river and enters the sea, the sea of stagnant waters. The waters will come fresh. Such is the power of this living water.

Everything will live where the river goes. This is where the great movement from death to life begins in the great sweep of the story of salvation. It begins with a prophet who has lived 25 years with the failure of his nation in which he shares. Yet his vision of God and the grace of God overcomes even the desert and the Dead Sea and the destruction of his nation. He is able to imagine a river of life which will overcome even death itself and change everything.

Jesus told the Samaritan woman at the well of this living water: "The water I will give will become in them a spring of water gushing up to eternal life."[10]

Each generation has its own challenges in the world economy and significant renewal is needed. As we seek to develop fresh vision, we need God's renewing grace and power.

It is not enough simply to prescribe new systems and solutions and tell each other what to do as if we knew. The only place to begin is by coming again to the living waters. We need to dig the wells, to unblock the springs of new life and open channels of blessing. We need to come to the place of prayer and sacrifice and stay long enough to notice what God is doing, the beginning of the river's source, new life. We need to come again to Christ and share the living waters which will flow from our hearts into the world around us.

I believe that when followers of Christ will be fully devoted to following Jesus in their economic lives, surrendering all to Him, these rivers of

---

10. John 4:14

living water, will flow and bring healing and life.

Read Ezekiel's vision.

"Then he brought me back to the door of the temple, and behold, water was issuing from below the threshold of the temple toward the east (for the temple faced east). The water was flowing down from below the south end of the threshold of the temple, south of the altar. Then he brought me out by way of the north gate and led me around on the outside to the outer gate that faces toward the east; and behold, the water was trickling out on the south side.

Going on eastward with a measuring line in his hand, the man measured a thousand cubits, and then led me through the water, and it was ankle-deep. Again he measured a thousand, and led me through the water, and it was knee-deep. Again he measured a thousand, and led me through the water, and it was waist-deep. Again he measured a thousand, and it was a river that I could not pass through, for the water had risen. It was deep enough to swim in, a river that could not be passed through. And he said to me, "Son of man, have you seen this?"

Then he led me back to the bank of the river. As I went back, I saw on the bank of the river very many trees on the one side and on the other. And he said to me, "This water flows toward the eastern region and goes down into the Arabah, and enters the sea; when the water flows into the sea, the water will become fresh. And wherever the river goes, every living creature that swarms will live, and there will be very many fish. For this water goes there, that the waters of the sea may become fresh; so everything will live where the river goes. Fishermen will stand beside the sea. From Engedi to Eneglaim it will be a place for the spreading of nets. Its fish will be of very many kinds, like the fish of the Great Sea. But its swamps and marshes will not become fresh; they are to be left for salt. And on the banks, on both sides of the river, there will grow all kinds of trees for food. Their leaves will not wither, nor their fruit fail, but they will bear fresh fruit every month, because the water for them flows from the sanctuary. Their fruit will be for food, and their leaves for healing."[11]

A Closing Prayer

Sir Francis Drake was an English sea captain who lived from 1540 - 1596. He was the second sailor to circumnavigate the globe. This is his famous prayer, one that it would appear God heard and rewarded. Let's make it ours today and see where God takes us!

Disturb us, Lord, when

We are too pleased with ourselves,

When our dreams have come true

Because we dreamed too little,

When we arrived safely

Because we sailed too close to the shore.

Disturb us, Lord, when

With the abundance of things we possess

We have lost our thirst

For the waters of life;

Having fallen in love with life,

We have ceased to dream of eternity

And in our efforts to build a new earth,

We have allowed our vision

Of the new Heaven to dim.

Disturb us, Lord, to dare more boldly,

---

11. Ezekiel 47:1-12

To venture on wilder seas

Where storms will show Your mastery;

Where losing sight of land,

We shall find the stars.

We ask you to push back

The horizons of our hopes;

And to push back the future

In strength, courage, hope, and love.

This we ask in the name of our Captain, Who is Jesus Christ.

Amen.

Disclaimer

In this book, we have used a lot of Biblical quotations. I have placed them in footnotes, to make the text read easier.

I do hope that I have got all references correctly specified. If not, please let me know!

After a conference, I received a thank-you note from a speaker who wanted to give a last blessing to our ministry. The meetings had gone very well ... or so I thought until getting his letter! He later qualified what he wanted to say, in quoting Acts 20:32. "Now I commit you to the Lord and to the word of His grace which is able to build you up ...". However, the verse he actually quoted was Acts 19:32, which says, "The assembly was in confusion: Some were shouting one thing; some another. Most of the people did not even know why they were there!"

Be careful when quoting a Bible reference! After reading this book, I hope Acts 20:32 is true for you, and not 19:32.

Anyway, my professor used to say, "If you cannot convince them, confuse them!" So I win both ways!

Peter J. Briscoe, Leiden, The Netherlands
Please feel free to mail me! peter@briscoe.nl

About Compass

Compass - finances God's way is a global, non-denominational movement teaching financial discipleship and generosity. The purpose is to serve churches, businesses, ministries, schools and other organisations by providing biblically based solutions on handling money and possessions. Our vision is to see everyone, everywhere faithfully living by God's financial principles in all areas of their lives.

Global mission

Compass' mission is to help people everywhere to learn, apply and teach Gods financial and business principles. We are looking for three major outcomes.

To know Christ more intimately as we trust and obey Him, experiencing Christ at work.

To become free from worry, fear, stress and anxiety and then be free to serve and love the Lord and our neighbours.

To contribute to fulfilling the Great Commission by giving our money and other resources to fund the work of the Church.

The Compass Global Team is comprised of local leadership on 6 continents – Europe, Asia, South America, North America, Africa and the Indian sub-continent. Our continental offices serve more than 90 nations around the world.

To get in touch, please visit the Compass Global landing page www.compass1.global

Resources

Compass has developed a wide range of resources in a wide variety of formats, such as DVD based teaching, workshops, small group studies, e-books and online learning.

There are teaching resources for all ages, from small children through students to adults; with application to areas of life such as business, church, marriage and family.

Compass is active in over 80 nations over the globe and has resources in many languages.

Contact our continental offices at www.compass1.global

To see specific English language resources, please visit the European shop at www.compass1.eu/shop; the US shop at www.compass1.org or the UK shop at www.yourmoneycounts.org.uk.

CPSIA information can be obtained
at www.ICGtesting.com
Printed in the USA
LVHW022042071019
633407LV00002B/127/P